South Africa 1880–1902

COMBAT

Boer Guerrilla
VERSUS
British Mounted Soldier

Ian Knight

First published in Great Britain in 2017 by Osprey Publishing,
PO Box 883, Oxford, OX1 9PL, UK
1385 Broadway, 5th Floor, New York, NY 10018, USA
E-mail: info@ospreypublishing.com

Osprey Publishing, part of Bloomsbury Publishing Plc

OSPREY is a trademark of Osprey Publishing, a division of Bloomsbury
Publishing Plc.

A CIP catalogue record for this book is available from the British Library.

Print ISBN: 978 1 4728 1829 4
PDF e-book ISBN: 978 1 4728 1830 0
ePub e-book ISBN: 978 1 4728 1831 7
XML ISBN: 978 1 4728 2329 8

Index by Rob Munro
Typeset in Univers, Sabon and Adobe Garamond Pro
Maps by bounford.com
Originated by PDQ Media, Bungay, UK
Printed in China through World Print Ltd.

17 18 19 20 21 10 9 8 7 6 5 4 3 2 1

Osprey Publishing supports the Woodland Trust, the UK's leading
woodland conservation charity. Between 2014 and 2018 our donations
are being spent on their Centenary Woods project in the UK.

To find out more about our authors and books visit
www.ospreypublishing.com. Here you will find extracts, author
interviews, details of forthcoming events and the option to sign up for
our newsletter.

Editor's note

Unless otherwise noted, all illustrations are from the author's collection.
Imperial measurements are used in this book. For ease of comparison
please refer to the following conversion table:

1 mile = 1.6km
1yd = 0.9m
1ft = 0.3m
1in = 2.54cm/25.4mm
1lb = 0.45kg

CONTENTS

Introduction

At about midday on 8 February 1881 a British civilian war correspondent, Thomas Carter, found himself on a low, rocky rise overlooking the Ingogo River in the British colony of Natal, in southern Africa, being shot at by the Boers. 'It was the first time I had been under fire', he recalled ruefully, 'and I confess that the sensation was not a pleasant one' (Carter 1900: 200). Carter had started out from camp that morning accompanying a small party of just under 400 British troops, led by Major-General Sir George Pomeroy Colley, who hoped to clear away small parties of the enemy who had been threatening Colley's lines of communication. Colley had marched about 6 miles, however, when he encountered about 150 Boers trying to block the road. As he deployed his men the Boers moved rapidly to surround him, and Colley had been forced to establish a defensive perimeter among a ring of rocks on a rise beside the road. Carter – who admitted he '"took earth" in the centre of the plateau' – made notes as the bullets 'came tearing with an angry buzzing sound through the short grass' (Carter 1900: 200) and provided a succinct summary of the day's events:

> Rifles, having lined the crest of this hill, kept up smart fire. Time, 12 noon. Boers returned fire hotly and from all sides of the hill, except rear. One of the 9-pounders facing right, the other left, pounded away for a good half hour … Among the gunners the casualties are very heavy … The firing is kept up in a desultory way, now dropping, now freshening up again. (Quoted in Norris-Newman 1882: 158)

For much of the battle Colley's troops were pinned down and anyone who stood in the open attracted a storm of well-directed fire. In the early afternoon Colley tried to break the deadlock by mounting a sharp flanking attack against the Boer positions. Carter witnessed it – and saw that it was soon over:

> To drive the Boers from their cover here, the mounted men, whose horses had already suffered a good deal, were ordered to charge. Major [William] Brownlow

Orange Free State General W.J. Kolbe in 1899. The only indication of his allegiance is a Free State rosette in his lapel and a coloured band around his hat, and his revolver offers the only hint of his rank. He is carrying a Mauser carbine. Boer officers seldom wore anything to distinguish themselves from their men. It had been fashionable for some commandants to turn out in clothes which reflected their civilian standing, particularly the long black coats and tall hats they wore to church, but this did not long survive the rigours of war in 1899. At the start of the Second Anglo-Boer War a few commandants from the Free State wore sashes in the Republic's colours – orange, red, blue, green and white – but these too did not survive long. Rather more successful were cockades or coloured ribbons or pressed-metal hat-badges based on each republic's coat of arms. Even these began to disappear as the conventional war gave way to guerrilla war, however, and the majority of burghers (citizens) on active service right across the period preferred to wear nothing distinctive at all.

of the K.D.G., their commander, with Lieutenant [John] Collinson, led the troop cheerily to the edge of the plateau, close by Parsons' gun, and over the side of the crest. Before the order to charge could be given, the Boers in this quarter, now not more than 150 yards distant, gave them a terrible volley, which, however, seemed directed mainly at their horses, for, although immediately half the men were dismounted, only one was wounded. (Carter 1900: 201)

The attack collapsed within minutes, and the battle settled once more into a firefight; only when night fell was Colley finally able to extricate his men. Brownlow's charge had seemed an almost insignificant incident in the battle and yet with hindsight it takes on an altogether different significance. Brownlow's men were a scratch force cobbled together to act as mounted infantry – to move on horseback but fire on foot. This was the way the Boers traditionally fought,

The Boer leader Piet Uys and his sons in 1879. Because of the egalitarian nature of Boer society, all decisions from strategy to daily duties were made through a council of war, in which every burgher (citizen) was as entitled to give his opinion as the commandant himself. Even so, peacetime standing and patronage remained an important factor – Uys was an influential frontier farmer and many of those who joined his commando were members of his extended family. He was one of the few Boer leaders to join the British during the Anglo-Zulu War, and was killed at the battle of Hlobane; the appearance of these men is typical of Boers in the field in the 1870s and 1880s.

but for the British in 1881 it was a relatively new concept and Brownlow, a cavalryman, had misunderstood its application, with disastrous consequences. Yet it pointed the way to the future of conflict in southern Africa, for by the time the Second Anglo-Boer War came to an end in 1902 'mounted infantry' tactics dominated the war on both sides, and from such a faltering beginning the British had largely become equal to their Boer counterparts.

The Boers were European settlers in southern Africa, descendants of a small colony established by the Dutch at the extreme southern tip of the continent in 1652. The Dutch settlement had gradually expanded into the interior, clashing with indigenous African societies along the way, and in 1806 control of the colony had passed to the British in one of the twists and turns which marked the progress of the Napoleonic Wars in Europe. Many of the settlers on the colony's frontiers – who were known by the Dutch word for farmer, *Boere* – found the British administration unsympathetic, however, and in 1836 there began an exodus from British territory known as the Great Trek.

The Great Trek reshaped the political geography of the interior of southern Africa. After a series of conflicts with African groups the Boers established two new republics: the Orange Free State (often shortened to Free State) and the South African Republic (usually known as the Transvaal). The British regarded the Boers as errant subjects, however, and there were a number of clashes in the 1840s as the British attempted unsuccessfully to reassert their authority. During the 1870s, however, the British adopted a concerted forward policy in southern Africa, and in 1877 annexed the Transvaal. The

Boers did not initially resist, but in December 1880 there was an uprising – known to later generations as the First Anglo-Boer War – and British garrisons in the Transvaal were cut off. Major-General Sir George Pomeroy Colley was deputed to march from Natal to relieve them, but lost a series of battles – including Ingogo (Schuinshoogte) – in early 1881 which culminated in his death on Majuba Hill on 27 February.

Colley's military failures led to Britain abandoning her claims to the Transvaal. With the discovery of gold in 1886, however, Britain again became involved in Transvaal affairs on the pretext of defending the rights of the many British miners who flocked there. The Boer government was unsympathetic to mining interests and in 1896 the mining magnate and prime minister of the Cape, Cecil Rhodes, attempted to organize a coup within the Transvaal, the so-called 'Jameson Raid'. The coup failed, however, and both Britain and the Transvaal prepared for open war, and the Free State allied itself with its fellow Boer republic. In October 1899 the Transvaal demanded that

British Regular mounted infantry retreating to Ladysmith after the withdrawal from Dundee in northern Natal at the beginning of the Second Anglo-Boer War. They are wearing greatcoats against the wet weather and carrying their rifles in the Namaqua bucket, held in place by a leather strap around the upper arm.

By the end of 1900 the primacy of British infantry was beginning to give way as the Second Anglo-Boer War had largely become a struggle between two armies fighting a mounted-infantry style of warfare. The Imperial Yeomanry – such as this man – were raised in the UK from among members of county Yeomanry regiments.

1 **20 December 1880:** Following the rebellion of the Transvaal Boers against the British annexation of the former republic, a column of British troops from the 94th Regiment, marching to reinforce the garrison in the capital, Pretoria, is attacked on the road at Bronkhorstspruit.

2 **28 January 1881:** Seeking to march from Natal to the aid of besieged British garrisons in the Transvaal but finding that Boer forces under Commandant-General Piet Joubert are blocking the route at the Laing's Nek Pass, British troops under Major-General Sir George Pomeroy Colley attempt to break through their lines at Laing's Nek, but are defeated.

3 **8 February 1881:** Colley's forces are bested again at Ingogo (Schuinshoogte).

4 **26–27 February 1881:** Colley's forces are defeated a third time at Majuba, with Colley himself being killed. A peace treaty is signed on 23 March and control of the Transvaal passes back to the Boers.

5 **October 1899:** Following years of further tension with the British, the Transvaal Republic launches a pre-emptive strike against British troops massing in southern Africa. The principal Boer thrust – again under Joubert – enters Natal via the Laing's Nek Pass. Joubert brushes aside British garrisons in northern Natal and surrounds the British concentration at Ladysmith. Boer forces also threaten the diamond-mining town of Kimberley in the west, the northern Cape Colony and the town of Mafikeng, which commands the British-held railroad going north.

6 **15 February 1900:** British forces massing in the northern Cape relieve Kimberley after heavy fighting, and push forward to occupy the Boer republics. With the fall of the Free State capital Bloemfontein (March 1900) and the Transvaal capital Pretoria (June 1900), the conventional phase of the war effectively comes to an end – after that, those Boers who continue to resist the British occupation do so as guerrillas.

7 **27 February 1900:** British troops under General Sir Redvers Buller eventually relieve Ladysmith after heavy fighting in a series of battles. Buller then drives the remaining Boer forces out of Natal.

8 **Mid-1900:** Boer guerrilla leaders such as Christiaan Rudolf de Wet in the Free State, Jacobus 'Koos' de la Rey in the western Transvaal and Louis Botha in the northern Transvaal start to mount an effective challenge to British control of the rural areas away from the main towns and railway lines, forcing the British to develop new strategies and tactics to combat them.

9 **6 November 1900:** Despite enjoying a particularly high reputation for daring and mobility, and slipping through the cumbersome British cordons many times, De Wet is caught by surprise and suffers a rare defeat at Bothaville (Doornkraal).

10 **September 1901:** Suffering heavily from the British strategy of tying down the veldt with chains of blockhouses and mobile columns, and by the practice of destroying farmhouses to deny them supplies, the Boers decide to try to reinvigorate the war by launching a number of raids deep into British-held territory. Assistant Commandant-General Jan Christian Smuts leads a mounted commando on a sweep south through the Transvaal and into the Cape Colony.

11 **17 September 1901:** Having skirmished constantly with British troops trying to intercept him, Smuts defeats a detachment of the 17th Lancers at Modderfontein (Elands River). Eventually reaching and surrounding the town of Okiep in the Western Cape, Smuts is still besieging Okiep on 26 April 1902 when he is summoned to take part in the peace negotiations at Vereeniging. The treaty signed at Vereeniging on 31 May 1902 brings the war to an end.

Britain withdraw its troops from the borders of its neighbouring colonies, and when Britain failed to comply Boer forces invaded British territory.

The resulting conflict, the Second Anglo-Boer War, lasted for three years. Although heavily outnumbered the Boers, who remained primarily an armed citizens' militia, posed the greatest challenge to British imperial might during the Victorian era, and it required the development of recognizably modern counter-insurgency strategies and tactics to defeat them. While these included the separation of combatant Boers from their civilian support base and physical restrictions on the landscape to hamper their movements, at the heart of these new strategies were mounted troops who were not reliant on tactics more suited to conventional European battlefields, but could challenge the Boers' superior mobility and yet still match their firepower.

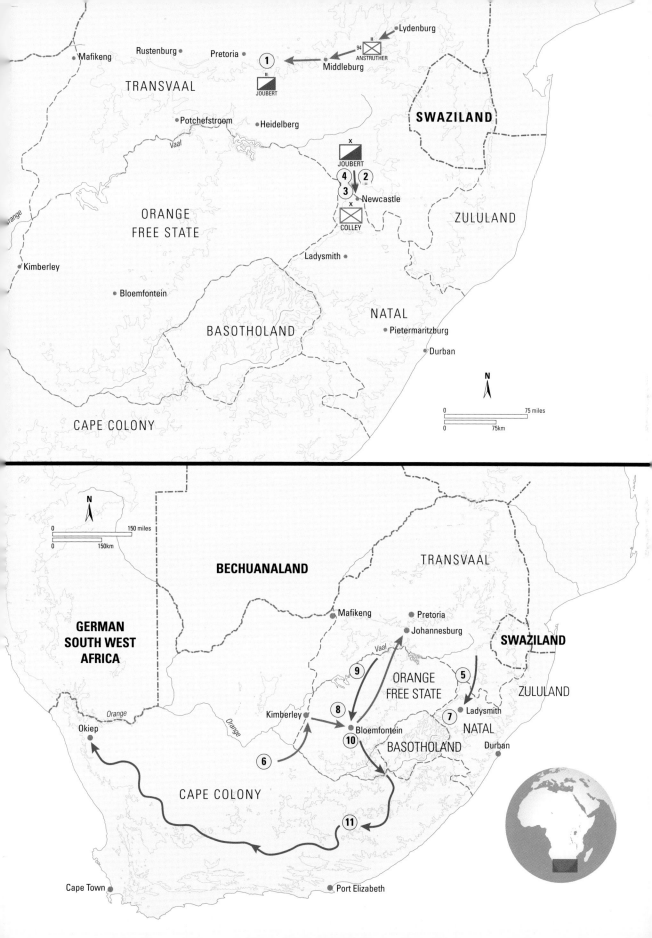

Lydenburg

Rustenburg • • Pretoria •

Mafikeng •

94
ANSTRUTHER

① Middleburg

TRANSVAAL

JOUBERT

SWAZILAND

Potchefstroom •   • Heidelberg

Vaal

ORANGE
FREE STATE

JOUBERT

④ ②
③
Newcastle

COLLEY

ZULULAND

Kimberley •

Ladysmith •

• Bloemfontein

BASOTHOLAND

NATAL

• Pietermaritzburg

• Durban

N

0   75 miles
0   75km

CAPE COLONY

N

0   150 miles
0   150km

BECHUANALAND

TRANSVAAL

Mafikeng •

• Pretoria

• Johannesburg

GERMAN
SOUTH WEST
AFRICA

Vaal

SWAZILAND

⑨

ORANGE
FREE STATE

⑤

ZULULAND

Orange

Okiep •

Orange

Kimberley •

⑧

⑦ • Ladysmith

⑥

• Bloemfontein

⑩

NATAL

• Durban

BASOTHOLAND

CAPE COLONY

⑪

Cape Town •

• Port Elizabeth

The Opposing Sides

ORIGINS AND ETHOS

Boer

With one or two exceptions towards the end of the period the Boers were never professional soldiers – they seldom wore uniforms, often provided their own weapons, were subject to very little discipline, and were in fact never more than an armed citizenry gathered together temporarily in defence of their interests or homes. Indeed, perhaps the overriding characteristic of the Boers was their independent spirit, and for much of the period they did not think of themselves as a unified people at all but rather identified themselves by largely local allegiances. The administration of the first colony at the

Two back-veldt Boers in 1881 – a picture which embodies some of the prejudices with which the British military regarded the non-professional Boer fighters during the First Anglo-Boer War. In 1881 the most popular style of dress for outdoor wear was a loose-fitting, double-breasted suit of hard-wearing yellow corduroy – which weathered after prolonged exposure to the sun and rain from a yellow ochre through to various shades of tobacco-colour – often worn with a waistcoat and a flannel shirt. Footwear at that time was usually the home-made leather *veldschoen* (field shoe). Photographs suggest that hats – essential to keep off the sun and the rain – still reflected the old *Voortrekker* taste for wide brims.
(De Agostini / Biblioteca Ambrosiana)

Cape may have been Dutch, but it accepted as settlers religious refugees from France and Germany, insisting only that they were followers of the Protestant faith. Living on farms widely separated from one another, used to feeding themselves and surviving in a harsh and sometimes inhospitable landscape, resentful of authority and not always speaking the same language as their neighbours, the early Boers were individualistic and self-reliant. A century of common experience, of a common desire for grazing land and livestock, of common hardships and common threats from outsiders including African ethnic groups and the British, gradually forged a sense of national identity but this was in its infancy, even during the Second Anglo-Boer War, and really only emerged in its recognizably modern form during the nationalist revival which marked the centenary of the Great Trek in the 1930s.

Instead, most Boers identified themselves as members of an extended group of a local community or district. Even so, they often quarrelled and disagreed among themselves, and the history of the Great Trek, for example,

A Boer commando in the field during the 1830s. The commando system evolved as a citizens' militia for the defence of frontier farmers and its basic principles did not vary much during the later wars against the British. As this picture suggests, mobility and firepower lay at the heart of the Boer military strength.

is marked by fissures and rivalries between Trek groups. Nevertheless, if most Boers were not motivated to fight by an abstract concept such as military glory, or even by an attachment to their country or government, they regularly took up arms in the cause of the perceived freedoms of their way of life, for their right to own farms, to live as they chose, and not be constrained by outsiders. What brought this disparate society together was either a common enemy or a common objective – to defend themselves against African resistance, to incorporate African lands or herds by military force, or (time and again throughout the period) to resist the imposition of British colonial authority. Indeed, for many Boers whose parents or grandparents had settled the Free State or the Transvaal to escape British authority during the years of the Great Trek the very idea of British rule remained anathema. In 1842, after the Boers had lost a struggle against the British for the country around Port Natal on the eastern coast, one Boer woman, Johanna Smit, defiantly proclaimed that she would walk back barefoot over the uKhahlamba mountains than submit to live under the British again.

Because the Dutch had allowed only Protestant settlers from Europe at the Cape, many Boers also shared a common faith, and there was strong support among them for the sterner Protestant churches, Lutherans and Calvinists, which encouraged an unpretentious communication with God which suited the Boers' individualistic approach. Many also felt that their faith placed them above the African peoples among whom they lived, and the Great Trek had encouraged among many of them the belief that they were a chosen people, and that their political and military actions were guided by the hand of God.

British

The British Army from the 17th to the 19th centuries was organized into distinct arms with specific tactical roles – infantry, cavalry and artillery, plus support services – but these changed and evolved across the Victorian period, particularly among the cavalry. The early distinction between 'light' (Lancers and Hussars) and 'heavy' cavalry (Dragoons and Dragoon Guards) was, even by the 1870s, largely irrelevant as both were expected to fulfil the same duties on the battlefield: scouting and reconnaissance, protecting the flanks and rear of an army on the march, and mounting shock attacks with the so-called *arme blanche*, the sword or the lance. Such an attack could be devastating when launched against an enemy unprepared for it, and the tactic of the

Mounted infantry were ideally suited to conditions in southern Africa and deployed in a number of minor campaigns during the 1880s and 1890s – here, the Mounted Company of 1st Battalion, The Welsh Regiment visit the old Anglo-Zulu War battlefield of iSandlwana in 1883. While the wearing of khaki had become standard in India since before the Second Anglo-Afghan War (1878–79), troops in southern Africa were among the last to give up their scarlet frocks and as late as 1888 members of the mounted company of 1st Battalion, The Royal Scots (Lothian Regiment) were wearing theirs in Zululand.

cavalry charge had hardly changed from the Napoleonic Wars – a regiment would attack in three lines with about 400yd between them and with the rear two lines providing support for the first. There were some spectacular cavalry charges across the Victorian period – at Balaclava, Ulundi in Zululand, Kassassin in Egypt and Omdurman in the Sudan, even at Elandslaagte during the opening stages of the Second Anglo-Boer War – but in fact they, too, were increasingly anachronistic, and the opportunities for them were increasingly rare. In many theatres of colonial warfare it was unusual to catch the enemy in sufficient concentration and in circumstances appropriate to a charge, and indeed the terrain was often too broken to facilitate it. Moreover, as Balaclava had demonstrated in the 1850s, charges against an enemy well-equipped with modern weapons could have disastrous consequences.

As a result, the cavalry training manual of 1874 placed greater emphasis on mounted troops skirmishing and even fighting on foot. This produced a bitter split between cavalry theorists, some of whom argued that fighting on foot was the preserve of infantry, and that it squandered the true skills of a cavalry regiment which lay in the *arme blanche*, while others argued that the future of cavalry lay as 'mounted infantry' – i.e. as troops who used their horses to increase their mobility but who then dismounted to fight on foot. These wrangles were to continue across the late Victorian period and throughout the conflicts with the Boers.

There was, too, a historic awareness of the need for a troop type which combined the best of both cavalry and infantry fighting techniques. As early as the battle of Naseby in 1645 a regiment of Dragoons in Parliament's New Model Army – Britain's first professional army – had advanced on horseback to secure a position on the enemy's flank but had then dismounted to fight on foot. Such a hybrid force was particularly useful in colonial warfare when commanders were often under-resourced (Britain's Imperial commitments meant that there were usually too few Regular cavalry regiments to go around) and the enemy was often highly mobile.

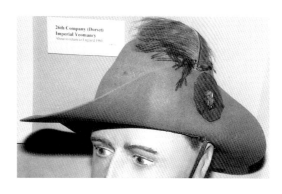

This was particularly true in southern Africa where as early as the first occupation of the Cape (1795–1802) a temporary cavalry company was raised from among the five infantry battalions based there to fight the local Xhosa people. Such units were designated as 'mounted infantry' – they lacked the finesse and *arme blanche* training of Regular cavalry, but instead used their horses to move around the battlefield and then dismounted to fight, often in open skirmishing formations. This was a type of warfare greatly suited to fighting both African enemies and the Boers, who were themselves both mobile and fighting in familiar terrain. Even after the British established a regiment to fight specifically on both horseback and on foot in southern Africa – the Cape Mounted Rifles – there was a continuing need to raise new ad hoc mounted infantry units. During the Ninth Cape Frontier War (1877–78), 300 mounted infantry were raised from four infantry battalions. These were designated, for the first time, as the 1st and 2nd squadrons of Imperial Mounted Infantry (IMI). They were disbanded after the Zulu and Pedi campaigns (1879), but the precedent was followed among infantry regiments stationed in the Transvaal on the eve of the First Anglo-Boer War and among the Natal Field Force. The mounted infantry would play a significant part in the First Anglo-Boer War, which would highlight both their strengths and weaknesses.

RECRUITMENT AND ORGANIZATION

Boer

The mechanism which brought the Boers together to fight was the commando system, which prevailed with only a few modifications across the period. Essentially a temporary levy of armed farmers, gathered together to serve as a military unit in the face of a particular emergency, it had emerged on the Eastern Cape Frontier from the late 18th century in the face of frequent clashes with the local Xhosa people. It imposed an obligation on all males within a given district to attend for service mounted on their own horses and carrying their own weapons, ammunition and supplies. Although successive administrations at the Cape accepted the responsibility to provide extra food and ammunition for prolonged service these units, called 'commandos', were seldom in the field for long, and often provisioned and indeed rewarded themselves from captured livestock. Although the legal basis for commando

The slouch hat would come to characterize the second half of the Second Anglo-Boer War on both sides. This example, with unit rosette and feather, belonged to the 26th Company (Dorset) Imperial Yeomanry. By 1899, all British troops were wearing khaki on active service, initially a light khaki cotton drill and later khaki serge which was heavier and darker. Mounted-infantry companies were issued with khaki breeches or pantaloons rather than trousers, but wore khaki puttees and infantry boots. Headgear was a khaki foreign-service helmet (either a white helmet with a khaki cover, or a khaki helmet) with, at the beginning of the war, a regimental flash at the side taken from the parent unit's shoulder-flash. These flashes were sufficiently conspicuous as to attract Boer fire, however, and they became smaller during the first year of the war and were eventually abandoned. During the guerrilla phase of the war many units abandoned their helmets altogether and replaced them with khaki slouch hats; at a time when some Boer commandos were forced to source new clothing from British prisoners, the Boers came to look increasingly like the British as the British came to resemble the Boers.

By late 1901 the 'bitter-ender' commandos still in the field were suffering the effects of the British war of attrition which had made resupply of essential articles almost impossible. Smuts' commando was composed of young men, inured to the hardships of life on campaign on the veldt by two years of war. Nevertheless, those hardships – of hard riding, living out in all weathers and too little food – can be read in his features and his unkempt appearance.

Weapons, dress and equipment

This Boer has managed to retain his Mauser rifle (**1**) – as some did, even to the end of the war – but besides the clip he is loading he has only one other clip of ammunition remaining in his bandolier (**2**), and in all probability he will take advantage of the Boer success at Modderfontein to abandon his Mauser in favour of a British Lee-Enfield rifle and British ammunition belts.

Although by 1899 Boer society had been subject to a small degree of urbanization, the majority of men still came from farms or small towns in the rural districts and wore hard-wearing farm clothes, perhaps home-made shoes (**3**), and wide-brimmed hats (**4**). Many men had started the war wearing rosettes or badges to denote their allegiance to the Free State or the Transvaal, but by 1901

this had largely fallen away. This man may decide to replace his ragged civilian coat (**5**) with a captured British jacket; this practice was becoming so prevalent that the British were worried that confusion on the battlefield was commonplace and had proclaimed that any Boer wearing captured British uniform would be shot. Indeed, at the beginning of the Modderfontein action a patrol of the 17th Lancers had mistaken some of Smuts' men who were wearing khaki items for British troops and had been taken by surprise as a result. Nevertheless, the practice would continue out of necessity until the end of the war – Deneys Reitz, who left a vivid account of Modderfontein, was able to largely re-clothe and re-equip himself from looted British kit after the battle.

service was not formally constituted – the South African Republic did not pass a formal commando law until 1898, on the eve of the Second Anglo-Boer War – the concept was widely understood and adhered to as a means of mutual support, particularly in sparsely settled areas where individual farmers were hard pushed to defend themselves alone.

All men between the ages of 16 and 60 were liable to commando service, but it was not unusual for boys under and old men over that age to take part as men often attended in family groups. Indeed, family patronage was a key element in commando service in the early years and the support or otherwise of a patriarch might determine the extent to which his family and dependents took part. Each commando elected its own commanding officer – its commandant – and again in the early days family patronage could be a key element in the choice of an officer. Men who had a good deal of influence within a community, and who were well-connected through family marriages, were often an obvious choice as leader, although whether they retained their authority would largely depend on how competent they proved to be. In prolonged campaigns there was a tendency for officers who had been elected on the strength of their position within civilian society but who proved to be poor military leaders in the field to be replaced and for individuals with greater leadership skills to rise and replace them.

Throughout the Great Trek period the Boers had defeated and displaced a number of African groups, and while some of these had been squeezed out of areas of Boer settlement enough remained to serve as labourers on Boer farms. Africans were not subject to direct commando service but were often required to accompany the farmer to act as servants, *agterryers* (grooms, tending the horses), wagon-drivers, herdsmen, cooks or labourers. During the Second Anglo-Boer War, which saw Boer society mobilized to an unprecedented degree, many thousands of Africans served with the Boer forces and played a prominent role in digging the Boer entrenchments which were a significant part of the early conventional stage of the war. Foreigners living within the Boer republics were, however, required to serve, and this became problematic following the discovery of gold in the Transvaal in 1886. Many thousands of *uitlanders* – outsiders – had flocked into the country during the gold rush but, fearing it might lose power to them the Transvaal government had refused to enfranchise them. They were nevertheless expected to serve under commando law and their resulting resentment was one of the issues seized upon by the British to justify their intervention in Transvaal affairs. Although most *uitlanders* left the Transvaal rather than fight the British a few came to identify themselves with their adoptive country and were willing to fight in its defence, so among the commandos in 1899 there were a number of Englishmen, Scots and Irishmen, as well as foreigners from other countries.

The muster of a Boer commando in a Free State town in 1899 on the eve of the Second Anglo-Boer War. Only the details of weapons and ammunition made this scene different from dozens similar in other towns in earlier wars across the 19th century. At first, commandos were simply raised in a town from among the townsfolk and the farmers in the outlying districts. As a result, their size depended on the region's population and the numbers were often quite small.

British

Recruitment into the Army reflected the class structure of contemporary British society. The ordinary soldiers were drawn from the rural or urban poor, and while some enlisted in the hope of adventure or to escape family complications at home most were simply forced to the Army by unemployment; although the standing of the Army within civilian society was low it did at least offer the prospect of an occupation, food, shelter, clothing and nominal payment. In 1870, in an attempt to broaden the appeal of Army service to a better class of recruit, enlistment was reduced from 12 years to six with the Colours and a further six on a newly created reserve, with an option to re-enlist. By the time of the First Anglo-Boer War in 1880–81, soldiers who had enlisted under the earlier long-service system had largely passed through the Army, and the short-service system was the norm for the rest of the period.

Throughout the period a cavalry regiment consisted of roughly 650 men, divided into four squadrons of 150 men each. In 1888 the mounted infantry were formally recognized by the establishment of two training schools in the UK, at Aldershot (later at Shorncliffe) and the Curragh. The mounted infantry were not to be constituted as a specific force, but rather the training schools were to provide a ten-week training course for detachments of one officer and 32 men from each of the infantry battalions stationed at home in the UK. Most mounted-infantry units had hitherto been organized on an ad hoc basis, but in addition to providing a trained group of mounted-infantry specialists within each infantry battalion the schools also established a blueprint for a mounted-infantry company with a total strength of 133 of all ranks. Such a company would be formed from the sections within each infantry battalion, and it was envisaged that on active service a number of such companies could be brigaded together to form a mounted-infantry battalion.

With the outbreak of the Second Anglo-Boer War the shortage of effective cavalry units again became apparent and more mounted-infantry units were hastily raised – a total of 28 Regular battalions by the end of the war. Even so, these would not be enough and they were supported by a large number of Yeomanry, Volunteer and colonial forces. The county Yeomanry regiments within the UK were raised for local defence and could not be deployed overseas, but a new force, the Imperial Yeomanry, was raised from volunteers from existing county units. The Imperial Yeomanry were organized into battalions, based on county affiliations, each consisting of four companies and a machine-gun section; a total of 526 men. A first detachment of 9,000 men was raised at the beginning of the war for a period of a year's service; when this expired a second detachment of 17,000 men was raised. In addition, British overseas colonies made a major contribution to the war effort – a total of 7,300 Canadians, 16,632

British Regular mounted infantry water their horses during one of the long sweeps across the veldt in pursuit of the Boer commandos which characterized the later stages of the Second Anglo-Boer War. Note the bayonet hanging from the waist-belt of the nearest man, and the forage bag.

Australians and 6,343 New Zealanders volunteered to serve in southern Africa, together with units of English-speaking South Africans and a handful of privately raised volunteer units. The vast majority of these were raised on an essentially mounted-infantry model, a type which, as the conventional phase of the Second Anglo Boer War came to an end, would increasingly dominate the battlefield for the rest of the war.

MORALE AND LOGISTICS

Boer

Despite the fact that it was nominally compulsory to attend a commando muster, there were always men who found excuses not to do so – and in a society which remained deeply suspicious of authority there were very few sanctions and little social stigma for those who chose not to do so. Wealthy men sometimes found proxies to serve in their place while some simply pleaded family commitments or pressing farm duties as an excuse. Most Boers were passionately attached to the idea that they were free burghers and not professional soldiers, and were moved to serve to defend their friends and relatives rather than by any call of military authority or discipline.

Although for the most part the majority of burghers fought in defence of their local interests, they were not immune to the chance to profit from their service. They were not paid but it was common in wars against African enemies for burghers to be allowed to keep any livestock they were able to seize, and some lucky Boers were able to make lasting improvements to their fortunes as farmers as a result. Indeed, it has been argued that the need for young Boers to acquire herds of their own outside the laws of family inheritance was a factor which drove some of the early conflicts with African enemies; and certainly it was not uncommon to promise that burghers would be rewarded with farms in captured territory at the end of a campaign.

The emphasis on local ties was both a strength and a weakness of the commando system. Burghers were motivated to fight out of a real need to support their local community; but at the same time they could fall prey to parochialism and were often uninfluenced by grand strategic designs which meant little to them, and morale often flagged if campaigns were waged for too long or too far away from home. In extreme circumstances commandos sometimes failed to support one another in a plan which seemed important to one but not the other. Having no commitment to a concept of military honour or glory, and recognizing instead the importance of individual survival to families left behind on distant farms, most burghers saw no shame in refusing to obey instructions if they were considered too dangerous or offered no obvious return.

Under such circumstances there was little recourse for commandants whose men refused to obey them, even in battle. The most effective commandants were those with natural leadership qualities who inspired their men through personal charisma and a sound record of success; men such as Jacobus 'Koos' de la Rey, Louis Botha and Jan Christian Smuts – although De la Rey did not stint on occasion to lay about him with his long rawhide *sjambok* whip.

Supplies for the Boer concentrations around Ladysmith at the end of 1899 arrive by ox-wagon. With little in the way of formal commissariat arrangements the supply of so many men was a haphazard affair; after the relief of Ladysmith and Kimberley it broke down entirely and during the subsequent guerrilla phase of the war the commandos had to forage for themselves. They were supported by sympathizers in the farming community, but this provoked the British to destroy Boer farms and remove non-combatants from the countryside.

For the most part, though, it was possible to exert only a minimal amount of discipline. On campaign routine duties were appointed but it was not unknown for burghers to refuse them or simply fail to turn up, even for important duties such as sentry duty at night in hostile territory. Punishments for such derelictions were mild by the standard of conventional armies and usually involved extra duties, fines or being tossed in a cowhide – a rough-and-ready piece of farmers' horseplay in which slits were cut in the side of a hide to serve as handles and the miscreant was bundled onto the hide then tossed repeatedly in the air by his comrades.

Supplying Boer commandos in the field was a perennial challenge. Since they were not a standing military force there was no established commissariat system and traditionally in the early days Boers attending a muster would bring their own provisions and expect to supplement them by living off the land. They did not, however, expect to be in the field for long, but even by 1880 warfare was becoming a more intense and protracted experience. Many Boers expected to take their ox-wagons on campaign with them, in which they loaded their own supplies and whatever luxuries they could gather to ameliorate life in the field. In the early wars against African enemies wagons provided an essential element of tactical defence, and the Boers would camp in laager, with their wagons linked together in a defensive circle. On several occasions during the Great Trek these laagers proved impregnable against even a determined attack by African enemies. In 1881 the Boers occupying positions around the Laing's Nek Pass were camped in a number of laagers to the rear, and even in 1899 many Boers turned out for duty with their wagons. The Boer forces which invaded northern Natal and the Cape Colony were accompanied by trains of hundreds of wagons. As attached as the Boers were to them, however, these wagons slowed the Boer advance and hampered one of their greatest assets, their mobility. After the relief of Kimberley in February 1900, General Piet Cronjé had withdrawn with all his wagons and had been pinned by a more nimble British pursuit against the banks of the Modder River where the futility of the laager as a method of defence against modern artillery and small arms had been woefully exposed. From that point commandos on all fronts began to abandon their reliance on ox-wagons; and although some clung to them until the bitter end, many commandos during

By this stage of the war indeed, with many Boers wearing captured British uniform and most British units wearing a variation on a universal uniform of khaki frock, riding breeches, slouch hat and bandoliers – the two sides were looking increasingly similar, and the sort of confusion which occurred at the beginning of the action at Modderfontein would continue until the end of the war. While British troops were resupplied with ammunition and worn kit, however, and went into battle with full bandoliers, the Boer 'bitter-enders' could only resupply themselves with items captured from their enemy.

Weapons, dress and equipment

In October 1900 the 17th Lancers' lances, carbines and swords were withdrawn in a move which acknowledged the limitations of *arme blanche* tactics against the Boers; they were replaced with the infantry Lee-Enfield rifle (**1**) which was more effective in the long-range firefights which typified the guerrilla war. Initially issued one 50-round ammunition bandolier (**2**), the regular cavalry – including the 17th Lancers – were then issued a second bandolier to support the increased reliance on the rifle and later, as here, a third webbing bandolier (**3**), which was worn around the waist.

The appearance of British regular cavalry had changed significantly over the course of the war. The khaki service frock (**4**) was worn with plain shoulder-straps in southern Africa rather than the shoulder chains issued in India. By Modderfontein the regiment's helmets had been withdrawn and replaced with the slouch hat (**5**), and the only conspicuous sign of regimental affiliation was a rosette badge (**6**) worn on the upturned brim of the hat which retained the regiment's home-service colours of dark-blue uniform with a white trim, and which carried the regiment's famous 'Death's Head' skull-and-crossbones motif.

Boer encampment at Colesberg, February 1900. Even by this stage of the war most seem to have re-equipped themselves with captured British Lee-Enfield rifles. Note the *biltong* – sun-dried strips of meat, a traditional Boer food – hanging from the line.

the guerrilla phase of the war relied purely on horses or at most upon light carts.

The Second Anglo-Boer War was by far the largest and most extended military commitment during the history of the republics, and it stretched the essentially temporary and haphazard supply system beyond breaking point. As warfare had become more protracted it was clearly impractical to expect large bodies of men to supply themselves indefinitely and the Transvaal Republic had agreed to shoulder the burden of feeding its commandos. In October 1899, however, some 40,000 Boers in all had answered the call to arms and the fragile commissariat system soon broke down. The government had bought up large quantities of livestock and the commandos advancing across the borders into British territory in October 1899 were accompanied by vast herds of sheep and cattle which they steadily consumed. The government undertook to supply bread, flour, coffee, sugar and salt and utilized the railway network to move them. In the early phase of the fighting, when Boer forces were investing British-held towns, supplies were sent to the front by train. From the railhead the supplies were supposed to be distributed by wagon, but arrangements were poor and inefficient, some commando camps being comfortably supplied while others received little or nothing. The Boer defeats in the early conventional phase of the war did at least free the Boer governments from the responsibility of supplying large quantities of men on fixed fronts, and once British counter-attacks had captured the capitals of the republics even that chain of supply broke down. As commandos became smaller and more manoeuvrable they grew more dependent on living off the land, either finding supplies among sympathetic farming communities, trading or raiding among African groups, or by hunting and gathering.

British

Unlike the essentially civilian militia system of the Boer republics, the British Army of the Victorian era was a full-time professional body whose members – at least for the lower ranks – lived largely apart from civilian society and under military law, were clothed, fed and armed by the Army, were trained to react to orders without question, and drilled to fight, until the very end of the period, in mass formations which neither required nor allowed individual initiative.

The life of a Victorian soldier was one of crushing routine. A recruit was taught to respond to orders, to stand and march correctly or, in a cavalry regiment, to ride, manage and care for his horse and to know his place in a line, and thereafter his regiment would frame his life throughout his service. He was housed in a barrack building which was often old, cramped, smoky and insanitary, and his days passed in a mind-numbing routine of drills and fatigues. For cavalrymen the daily need to muck out, feed and groom their horses added to the burden of their duties. Any dereliction of duty was likely to be sternly punished. If his unit was posted around the Empire he might be housed in an equivalent barracks abroad, but as often as not he would be expected to live under canvas sharing a large bell tent with 10–12 comrades, lying on a blanket on the ground with their feet towards the tent-pole, like the spokes of a wheel.

Army pay for ordinary soldiers was a shilling a day (slightly more for a cavalryman, to account for the extra needs of his horse) and subject to 'stoppages' – these were deductions to recover the cost of various necessities or lost or replaced kit and often amounted to the majority of his weekly pay. The daily food allowance was 1lb of bread and 12oz of meat with additional potatoes, salt, sugar and fresh vegetables where available. Although attempts were made to improve educational standards across the period, levels of illiteracy remained high and with little else to distract them most soldiers took solace in tobacco and alcohol. Indeed, the capacity of the ordinary British soldier to drink was legendary, and many soldiers spent what little pay they received entirely on alcohol. Throughout the 1870s the Army authorities had attempted to wean them from this fixation by supplying day rooms for recreational pursuits, libraries and basic educational facilities, and by encouraging participation in sports. Even so, drunkenness would remain a problem across the period.

The lives of officers had little in common with those of their men. They were drawn from the upper levels of society, mostly from the minor land-owning gentry, and were educated men who were allowed long periods of leave away from their regiments, and who therefore retained their links with civilian society and civilian pursuits. Although the purchase of commissions had been abolished before the First Anglo-Boer War, life as an officer still required a degree of wealth far beyond that of the men in the ranks. This was particularly true in cavalry regiments which for the most part considered themselves a social as well as a military elite, and some of which aspired to a particularly 'smart' or fashionable lifestyle; a cavalry officer was required to provide and support his own horses (at least two thoroughbreds), to pay for his own uniform, and as often as not to enjoy a conspicuously lavish lifestyle in keeping with his regiment's reputation. Officers lived separately from their men in a different 'officers' mess' building within the barracks; while junior officers might share two to a room, most

Life on the veldt: (left) a British field kitchen in the open air, and (right) a Yeomanry officer snatching a brief rest during a break in the interminable sweeps across country during the latter stages of the Second Anglo-Boer War.

officers had their own rooms. Since only a few officers were required to supervise drills and fatigues each day or to supervise musketry instruction, most of them spent little time with their men.

It was under these circumstances that the symbols of a common allegiance assumed such importance. Each regiment was proud of its history and traditions and each infantry battalion carried a pair of Colours (flags) which embodied not only their loyalty to the Crown but the past glories and battle honours of their regiment. To lose a Colour was a great disgrace although by the 1870s carrying Colours into battle was increasingly an anachronism, and indeed cavalry regiments had already ceased to carry Standards (their equivalent of Colours) into action. Nevertheless, the sense of regimental identity was further encouraged by distinctive elements on the uniform – 'facing' colours on the collars and cuffs, braided jackets for Hussar regiments or plastron fronts for Lancers – and by particular traditions within the regiment. All of these inculcated a sense of *esprit de corps* which both officers and other ranks alike were encouraged to live up to. In the final analysis while British soldiers did possess a sense of patriotism, of duty to Queen and country, this was rather more distant to them than their sense of loyalty to the regimental family, and it was the fear of letting their comrades down and dishonouring that family name which most often produced the greatest feats from them. At the same time it was a system which inculcated an innate conservatism, of finding strength in the familiar, which mitigated against radical change and which meant that new concepts, such as the mounted infantry, remained ad hoc and often temporary groupings long after their effectiveness had been validated in the field.

TRAINING, WEAPONS AND TACTICS

Boer

The 1895-pattern Mauser rifle was purchased by the Boer republics in large numbers and issued to the commandos on the eve of the Second Anglo-Boer War. It had an internal magazine which held five 7mm smokeless rounds loaded from a clip and was quick, accurate and ideally suited to the Boer way of fighting.

Because they were not a regular professional army the Boers did not have any formal military training. For much of the 19th century most Boers lived a rural lifestyle, growing up on farms which were often a day's ride from their neighbours. Individual Boers were accustomed to life in the open air, and knew and understood the southern African terrain and its moods, the baking heat of the summer days and the frosts of winter nights, the long periods without rain and the sudden storms and heavy deluges when those rains came. They understood the way that rivers which had dried almost to a trickle could rise and burst their banks within hours in response to a storm in the mountains many miles away, how to hunt for food and sun-dry meat to make it last, and the risks of Africa's wildlife. They were accustomed

to spending long days in the saddle, covering great distances in an easy, long-legged, comfortable ride, knew to watch out for the holes caused by ant-bears (*aardvarks*), and how to stay in the saddle when the horse shied at a snake or a hidden animal.

They knew, too, how to shoot. Few Boers were professional hunters but their shooting was practised and practical and honed by the experience of regularly shooting for the pot. When cartridges were expensive and sometimes difficult to come by, many Boers learned how to kill moving prey quickly and efficiently; and perhaps more important they learned to judge distance effectively, especially those who lived in the clear air of the high-veldt interior. It was this that made them superior to their professional British counterparts, for although Boer marksmanship has been over-mythologized, and many British soldiers were excellent shots over set distances, the Boers were generally more experienced in practical shooting, knew their weapons intimately, and were far better at judging moving targets at a distance.

There were, even so, changes in the nature of Boer society across the 19th century. Both the Free State and the Transvaal were settled by Boer families who had travelled great distances in their ox-wagons, fording rivers and crossing mountain ranges, and as often as not fighting African enemies along the way. By the 1860s, however, except for a few remote areas on the periphery of the republics, the great trekking days were over and Boer society, while almost entirely rural, was increasingly static. Most of the Boer commandos who fought in 1881 were the sons of Trekkers, and not Trekkers themselves, and hailed from farms in settled communities. This trend became more pronounced with the discovery of gold in the 1880s which attracted *uitlanders* who not only worked the gold-fields but provided shops and services for those who did – towns became larger, and the nascent urbanization had an effect on all but the most remote rural communities. By 1899 a small but significant proportion of the Boer forces came from towns and were by no means always the hardy back-veldt farmers of popular myth.

Until the eve of the Second Anglo-Boer War, Boers provided their own weapons. Guns could be expensive and difficult to replace and once a farmer became familiar with his weapon and attuned to its strengths and failings, he was often reluctant to part with it. Thus some elderly Boers turned out for commando duty in 1880 carrying the long-barrelled flintlock guns which had served them in their youth; some had muzzle-loading rifles of the 1850s. Most, by then, preferred breech-loading rifles, however, among which there was considerable variation, since they were all privately procured. Some preferred the .577-calibre Snider – essentially a breech-loading conversion of an earlier muzzle-loader – or the Westley-Richards 'Monkey-Tail', so-called because of a lever which hinged upwards to open the breech. These rifles fired lead bullets from greased paper-cartridges which were easy to manufacture on the farm. More popular, however, were weapons which fired rounds with brass cartridges, which were more robust for life on the veldt and were less vulnerable to damp and damage. The .500/.450 Westley-Richards falling-block rifle (known as the 'Free State Martini') and the .577/.450 Martini-Henry rifle were particularly popular in either the full-length version or the shorter carbine (which was lighter and easier to use on horseback). Men with older weapons which fired paper cartridges carried the rounds in cartouche-boxes or in their pockets while those who preferred brass-cartridge weapons carried their ammunition in leather bandoliers which held 50 rounds in single loops. Some men wore waistcoats with loops stitched in to hold single rounds.

All of these weapons fired black-powder propellant which produced great quantities of white smoke, but by the 1890s they had been superseded by magazine rifles which were quicker to load and which fired smokeless powder. In the aftermath of the Jameson Raid the Transvaal government imported 25,000 German 7mm Mauser rifles and ten million rounds of ammunition; these proved so popular in trials that a further order was placed, and soon afterwards the Free State followed the Transvaal's example. These weapons – together with a smaller number of other models, such as the Portuguese single-shot Guedes and British magazine Lee-Metford – were distributed when the commandos assembled in 1899. Where possible they were exchanged for the firearm already in the burgher's possession. It is a myth, therefore, that the majority of Boer commandos were long experienced with their weapons at the beginning of the Second Anglo-Boer War, since the majority had only just received them. The Mauser was, however, a light, easy-to-use and accurate rifle and became the signature weapon of the Boer commandos. With the outbreak of the guerrilla war from 1901, however, most Boer commandos found it increasingly difficult to procure fresh supplies of Mauser ammunition, and they began to turn instead to British .303 Lee-Enfields which, together with their ammunition, could be captured in battle or looted from British supply trains.

The Mauser was certainly well-suited to the challenges the war would place on it. It had an internal magazine which held five 7mm smokeless rounds loaded from a clip and a calm marksman could achieve a high rate of fire from a position which would not be betrayed by smoke. Rounds were carried in clips of five for ease of loading, often in a leather bandolier which took 10–12 clips in pouches, although a wide variety of other means of carrying

A group of Boers in a shelter outside Ladysmith at the beginning of 1900, looking resolute for the camera. Most of them are carrying Mauser rifles, but a couple appear to have the Portuguese 1885-pattern single-shot Guedes rifle, which was also purchased by the Transvaal Republic. By the 1890s the old yellow corduroy had largely disappeared, and the influx of traders to meet the booming gold market meant that a wider range of clothing was available. At the start of the Second Anglo-Boer War most Boers wore single-breasted jackets and trousers in various shades of brown or grey or muted blues. Hats with narrower brims were more fashionable, and many boots or shoes had replaced the home-made *veldschoen* among all but those who still lived on remote farms. As the Second Anglo-Boer War progressed, clothing became worn out and torn by long years spent living outdoors, and as the British steadily captured all the municipal centres it became difficult to acquire fresh supplies. Instead, many Boer commandos during the last stages of the guerrilla war – the so-called 'bitter-enders' – clothed themselves in the khaki uniforms of British prisoners. At times it became difficult to tell the two sides apart and at one point the British authorities authorized the shooting of captured Boers wearing British uniform as spies in an attempt to discourage the practice.

Boers taking shelter among rocky outcrops during the Second Anglo-Boer War, with their horses in the hollow behind. Once on foot, their tactics were essentially those of skirmishers: advancing in no particular formation, keeping dispersed and moving from cover to cover in southern Africa's rocky landscape, firing as they went. Most Boers had a good understanding of the terrain and were able to spot elements of the landscape which might give them a tactical advantage. Lacking the training, discipline or code of military honour to support the casualties that were an inevitable result of mass attacks at close quarters, they would seldom engage in hand-to-hand combat but would instead advance as close to the enemy as they could – sometimes as close as 20–30yd – and engage in an intense firefight. It was a style of warfare which had developed precisely to suit the circumstances and the terrain, and so effective was it that it came to dominate the Second Anglo-Boer War as the British also recognized its advantages and greatly increased their own mounted-infantry capability.

clips were employed ranging from bandoliers of webbing to waistcoats with special pockets for the clips.

In fighting African enemies the Boer commandos either launched a mounted attack, firing from the saddle and trusting to their greater speed and firepower to overcome a more numerous enemy, or fought from behind a defensive laager. Warfare against the British required different skills, however, since the British possessed a formidable firepower of their own and in order to neutralize it effectively the Boers needed to exploit their advantages in manoeuvrability, marksmanship and field craft. In defence, both in 1881 and in the early stages of the Second Anglo-Boer War, the Boers would carefully prepare defensive lines of trenches and stone breastworks which provided effective protection against British artillery and which rendered the approaches a killing-zone raked by rifle fire. In attack, although the Boers sometimes mounted charges from horseback, they preferred to advance rapidly on their objective then dismount and fight on foot. This was the essence of a tactical approach which the British, with their more formal and organized approach to soldiering, would categorize as one of 'mounted infantry'. Because individual Boers were mostly familiar with their own horses and had often trained them to stand and wait for their return when they dismounted, they required no formal system of horse-holders as conventional troops did, utilizing at the most a few African servants as horse-guards. This freed the majority of the Boers for fighting.

British

Until the very end of the period, the late-Victorian cavalryman was equipped to fight on both horseback and on foot. Those regiments designated as Lancers carried a 9ft bamboo lance with a steel tip and a red-over-white pennon as well as the sword and carbine carried by Hussar, Dragoon and Dragoon Guard regiments. During the First Anglo-Boer War the carbine was the single-shot Martini-Henry, but from 1889 these were replaced with the magazine Lee-Metford. The lance was impractical for use on foot, but the carbine at least allowed a cavalryman to fight dismounted, although it lacked the range of the infantry rifle. There were practical problems, too, as Lord Roberts noted during the Second Anglo-Afghan War (1878–80); the

A British mounted infantryman at Captain Henry Hallam Parr's training school in Pietermaritzburg, c.1881. The school was the first attempt to develop specific mounted-infantry skills and influenced the development of the concept in the run-up to the Second Anglo-Boer War. This man is wearing a typical field uniform for mounted infantry of the period: a scarlet undress frock from his parent unit, cord breeches and bandolier. His Martini-Henry rifle would normally be carried in the leather Namaqua bucket strapped to the saddle. In 1879 the IMI had been armed with the Swinburne-Henry carbine (the mounted equivalent, at that time, of the infantry's Martini-Henry rifle); ammunition was carried in a leather bandolier which held 50 individual rounds in loops. During the First Anglo-Boer War the men of Brownlow's Mounted Squadron were armed with Martini-Henry carbines, which had by now superseded the Swinburne-Henrys, and were deployed at Laing's Nek (28 January 1881) and Ingogo. Brownlow's force was small, however – just 130 men in total, of whom 119 were deployed at Laing's Nek and only 44 at Ingogo – and its showing was poor overall, largely because Brownlow himself preferred to fight as a cavalryman and attacked on both occasions on horseback rather than on foot.

cavalry were hampered when fighting on foot by their swords hanging from the waist-belts, which dangled between their legs, and by the fact that their carbines were carried muzzle-down in buckets on their horses and could be difficult to retrieve when dismounting. From 1891 swords were no longer worn on the waist-belt but were attached to the saddle and there were other changes, too. In the 1880s cavalry regiments went into action wearing home-service uniforms (scarlet or blue frocks) only modified by the adoption of a 'foreign service' helmet (only in India were khaki service uniforms approved for field use). This was, however, beginning to change: during the First Anglo-Boer War troops who had been based in southern Africa at the start of the war were still wearing scarlet while reinforcements shipped from Afghanistan were in khaki; by the time the Second Anglo-Boer War broke out in 1899 all British arms were wearing khaki. Even so, the impracticality of the *arme blanche* became apparent as the war progressed, and most cavalry regiments abandoned their helmets for wide-brimmed hats and traded their lances and swords for infantry Lee-Enfield rifles.

After the First Anglo-Boer War there was a move to incorporate mounted infantry as a permanent element in the Army. The first proper mounted-infantry school was established in the Natal colonial capital, Pietermaritzburg. This school trained volunteers from infantry battalions in proper mounted-infantry techniques including both horse management and appropriate tactics, and for the first time they were issued with equipment specifically designed for their role – a leather bucket, called the 'Namaqua bucket', attached to the saddle which hung behind the right leg and secured the butt of the carbine. Small numbers of mounted infantry trained at this school were deployed in Egypt in 1882, Zululand in 1888 and Suakin in the Sudan and, while some proponents of traditional cavalry continued to resist them, their role was finally recognized in 1888 by the establishment of the two UK training schools. These provided ten-week training courses for detachments from each infantry battalion who returned to their parent units at the completion of the course, but who could then be rapidly mobilized when a large mounted-infantry force was required. Because mounted-infantry tactics involved a greater degree of self-reliance than conventional infantry tactics, each detachment was divided into groups of four who worked together, choosing among themselves one man as leader. One man in each 'four' held the horses while the others dismounted to fight. This effectively reduced the fighting strength of a given mounted-infantry unit by a quarter, but it was widely held that four horses were the most an individual could comfortably manage and that a small number facilitated rapid mounting and dismounting. At the end of the mounted-infantry course the men returned to their parent battalions and resumed their duties as infantry, although they continued to train as mounted infantry during manoeuvres. In the field they were to wear khaki uniforms and were armed with the bolt-action magazine Lee-Metford (later Lee-Enfield) rifle, with rounds carried in leather bandoliers.

In the conventional phase of the Second Anglo-Boer War mounted-infantry units were deployed as scouts

By the 1890s a formally constituted system of raising a mounted-infantry detachment from each British line-infantry battalion had been implemented – this is Sergeant Seymour of 2nd Battalion, The Gordon Highlanders at Aldershot prior to departing to southern Africa for the Ndebele Rebellion in 1896. Note that the Namaqua bucket has been modified from the earlier deeper pattern to accommodate the magazine-loading Lee-Metford rifle. In the field the white jacket and forage cap were replaced with khaki.

and used to support infantry attacks. During the guerrilla war, however, they would become a central part of British strategy in an attempt to pin down the wide-ranging Boer commandos. The British erected lines of blockhouses across the country, linked by barbed-wire fences, and then orchestrated sweeps through the country in between, trying to pin the Boers against these lines. Although mobile British columns consisted of all arms, the increased reliance on mounted-infantry units gave them an extra speed and reach that enabled them at times to achieve some striking results.

Imperial Yeomanry in action; although the British abandoned the formal tactics with which they had begun the Second Anglo-Boer War, giving greater emphasis to mounted-infantry warfare – dismounting to fight in open formations from behind cover, as here – they never quite mastered the landscape as the Boers did, and the need for one man to remain behind the line with four horses reduced their potential firepower.

Ingogo
(Schuinshoogte)

8 February 1881

BACKGROUND TO BATTLE

In 1877 Britain annexed the Transvaal Republic as part of a new forward policy designed to impose a common British administration over southern Africa. Throughout 1880 there was growing pressure from the Boers to restore the Republic, but many British officers – including Major-General Sir George Pomeroy Colley, High Commissioner for South-Eastern Africa since July 1880 – believed that the Boers were too disorganized and undisciplined ever to prove a threat to professional British troops. After weeks of rising tension, however, on 16 December over-enthusiastic Republicans exchanged shots with the British garrison at Potchefstroom and the First Anglo-Boer War began.

The British hastily moved to concentrate their forces at Pretoria. In late November Lieutenant-Colonel Philip Anstruther had been ordered to march to reinforce Pretoria with his garrison (268 officers and men of the 94th Regiment) from Lydenburg, over 180 miles away. By 20 December Anstruther was near the town of Bronkhorstspruit when a party of Boers delivered a message from the provisional government instructing him to halt his march. Anstruther replied that he would continue in accordance with his orders. As he returned to the troops he noticed that the Boers were deploying on foot down the length of his column. Recognizing the danger, Anstruther ordered one of the 94th Regiment's companies to extend in skirmishing order; as they began the movement, however, the Boers opened fire. Within just 15 minutes, 156 men and one woman were killed or wounded. Anstruther – who was shot five times in the legs himself, and would die six days later – had no choice but to surrender.

News of his fate galvanized the British. The Boers had effectively shut down the Transvaal and isolated the elements of British control and it was

clear to Colley – who was both senior military and civil commander in southern Africa – that the only real hope of restoring British prestige was to march to their assistance. Throughout January 1881 he assembled a force in the neighbouring British territory of Natal: a total of 1,462 men of all ranks, including infantry, artillery and a Royal Navy detachment.

From the outset Colley was desperately short of cavalry. Although the Natal government allowed him control of the professional Natal Mounted Police, Colley was wary of using them too prominently for fear of poisoning the future relationship between British settlers and Boers, and for the same reason he did not call out the Natal Volunteer units. All Colley had left to serve as cavalry was a Mounted Squadron hastily cobbled together for the occasion. At the heart of the Mounted Squadron were 35 professional cavalrymen of the 1st (King's) Dragoon Guards who had been left behind on various duties when the rest of their regiment had left after the Anglo-Zulu War. They were bolstered by 25 men of the Army Service Corps and 60 mounted infantrymen drawn from the 58th Regiment and 3/60th Rifles. Mounted infantry had been deployed in Zululand to good effect but it was not entirely clear whether the Mounted Squadron was to serve in that role or as substitute cavalry, although Colley appointed a cavalry officer, Major William Brownlow of the 1st (King's) Dragoon Guards, to command it.

While Colley was preparing his forces, about 1,000 Transvaalers under the command of Commandant-General Piet Joubert moved to block the main road from Natal to the Transvaal, which rose up steeply through the foothills of the uKhahlamba (Drakensberg) mountains by way of a pass known as Laing's Nek. Joubert's men reached the pass ahead of Colley and occupied it, building shallow entrenchments on the ridges flanking it which gave them command of the approaches. Well aware of the urgent need to relieve the Transvaal garrisons, Colley decided to mount an immediate attack to clear the pass. He drew his troops up at the foot of the ridge occupied by the Boers and at 0915hrs on 28 January 1881 ordered his artillery to begin bombarding the Boer positions. It was the first time the Transvaalers had experienced an

The 58th Regiment attacks Laing's Nek with Colours flying, 28 January 1881. The attack marked a clear break with British military tradition, painfully demonstrating that a frontal assault in the open in red coats was no longer viable against a partially concealed enemy equipped with modern firearms.

artillery bombardment and they were undoubtedly unsettled by the shrapnel shells bursting above them, but as they crouched in their shallow trenches they soon realized that they were only really in danger from a direct hit, and their nerve held.

Colley then ordered the 58th Regiment to attack, with the Mounted Squadron protecting the infantry's right flank. As the 58th Regiment pushed up the slope it came under fire from a spur on the British right and Brownlow changed direction to counter the threat, but instead of employing his men like mounted infantry – dismounting and advancing on foot – he, like Colley, placed his faith in the moral effect of the charge. His men were deployed in two troops and as they changed direction one, composed largely of Dragoon Guards, drew ahead of the other

… in a most plucky way, in spite of the hill being like the side of a house. When they got to the top they found the Boers intrenched, and a tremendous fire greeted them, they had to retire with the loss of nineteen killed, wounded and missing. One man actually jumped his horse into the Boer intrenchment, and cut a man down; but he was shot dead the next moment. Two of the officers had great shaves; they both had their horses shot under them. One officer had a knife he carried tied to a belt around his waist shot to atoms and another bullet went under his arm and through his coat without hitting him. Another had the handle of his sword shot away. They were about six yards from the Boers, who potted at them as they ran down the hill for half a mile. (Quoted in Emery 1986: 105)

Joubert himself was apparently shocked by the fierceness of the brief mêlée, commenting that the mounted men 'came so close that the powder burned each other' (quoted in Norris-Newman 1882: 152), but the British could not hold their ground and were forced to retreat. Coming up behind them, the second troop refused to press home and the Mounted Squadron fell back in disarray. One officer who had his horse shot under him admitted ruefully that 'I got up, and, seeing no one about, I turned and legged it down the hill. My helmet had fallen off, my sword dropped out of my hand, and I lost my field-glasses. It was a dashed expensive day' (quoted in Lehmann 1972: 152).

The rout of the Mounted Squadron left the 58th Regiment's attack fully exposed to fire from the Boer trenches:

> Their men were hustled up at a tremendous pace, without even being extended in skirmishing order, up a hill tremendously steep, and over very rough ground; and the consequence was when they got near the top they were so blown they could hardly move; some of them couldn't even lift their rifles; and there was about 120 yards between their head and tail. A tremendous fire met them about 200 yards from the top of the hill, and there they stood, simply falling just like cut-down corn. It was a regular butchery. The Boers were quite fresh, and had the advantage of position and shooting down hill. (Quoted in Emery 1986: 105)

The repulse was complete and Colley's losses were heavy: seven officers and 77 men killed and three officers and 110 men wounded. The majority of these were from the 58th Regiment, but the Mounted Squadron had suffered heavily too: four men killed and 13 wounded, with 34 of their horses killed. Brownlow was apparently so disgusted by the failure of his second troop to charge home that he refused to speak to them that night back at the camp, but in fact their failure had more to do with confusion over their role than with any personal failings. Joubert admitted to 16 Boers killed and 27 wounded, mostly by Colley's artillery.

'Floreat Etona!' An incident during the battle of Laing's Nek – two British officers, both former pupils at Eton school, rush to the front during the attack by the 58th Regiment and are shot down. The scene was much the same during Major William Brownlow's ill-fated attack with the Mounted Squadron.

MAP KEY

1 Midday: Having set out to clear away Boers who were threatening his lines of communications from Mount Prospect camp to Newcastle, Major-General Sir George Pomeroy Colley sees a Boer force (under Field Commandant-General Nicolaas Smit) approaching on his right. The Boers advance to occupy a hollow to Colley's left and dismount, skirmishing forward through boulders and long grass.

2 c.1215hrs: Colley occupies a rise across the road, deploying his men behind the cover of patches of boulders where the edges of the summit fall away. A protracted firefight then ensues, with the British largely pinned down.

3 c.1300hrs: In an attempt to break the stalemate, Colley orders his Mounted Squadron, commanded by Major William Brownlow, forward from the shelter of the centre of the rise and directs them to attack the Boer flank opposite. Brownlow attempts to deploy for a conventional cavalry charge, but as he does so he exposes his men to a heavy Boer fire which is directed particularly at the horses. Brownlow's charge collapses in confusion and he is forced to withdraw.

4 1500hrs: By this time, having taken advantage of the slight hollows surrounding the British position steadily to surround it, the Boers have almost encircled their opponents.

5 c.1500hrs: In an attempt to prevent the Boers from completing this move, Colley despatches a half-company of the 3/60th Rifles under Captain J.C. MacGregor to check the Boers. MacGregor advances too far – he manages to halt the Boer advance but suffers heavy casualties and is himself killed. Colley remains pinned down on the plateau throughout the rest of the afternoon, but manages to withdraw under the cover of darkness.

Battlefield environment

The position Colley occupied was on the summit of a low triangular rise which falls away gently towards the east but rather more steeply towards the Ingogo River in the west. The top of the rise is largely open and almost flat, but the elements have exposed broken lines of boulders at various points as the ground slopes down. These provided Colley with a natural perimeter where his men could take cover, although for the most part the rocks themselves are seldom more than waist-high and lying or kneeling behind them for hours on end became a test of endurance. Down the slopes to the east, where Smit's men first attacked, the same rows of boulders poked out from the grass too far away for Colley to occupy, thereby providing excellent cover for the Boers as they skirmished forward.

On the opposite side, where the Boers gradually extended to surround the British position, there are fewer boulders, but in the damp hollows the grass was more than long enough to obscure the movements of men who knew how to make the most of the ground. From most of the Boer positions the British troops lining their perimeter would have been on the skyline slightly above them, and it was difficult to see anyone moving about on the centre of the rise beyond. This enabled Brownlow's Mounted Squadron to remain relatively safe as they awaited their orders, but in order to attack they first had to move to the edge of the rise where they were immediately exposed to Boer fire. As undramatic as the battlefield seems, Colley's decision to defend the rise left him vulnerable to encirclement and with no way of checking this beyond exposing his men to a well-directed fire from Boers who increasingly commanded all the approaches.

The battlefield of Ingogo (Schuinshoogte) in the 1890s, with the monument and graves on the rise held by the British. The view is from the Boer right, where the ground was more open and grassy; beyond the summit the ground falls away more steeply and is scattered with rocky outcrops. The hill on the right of the skyline is Majuba.

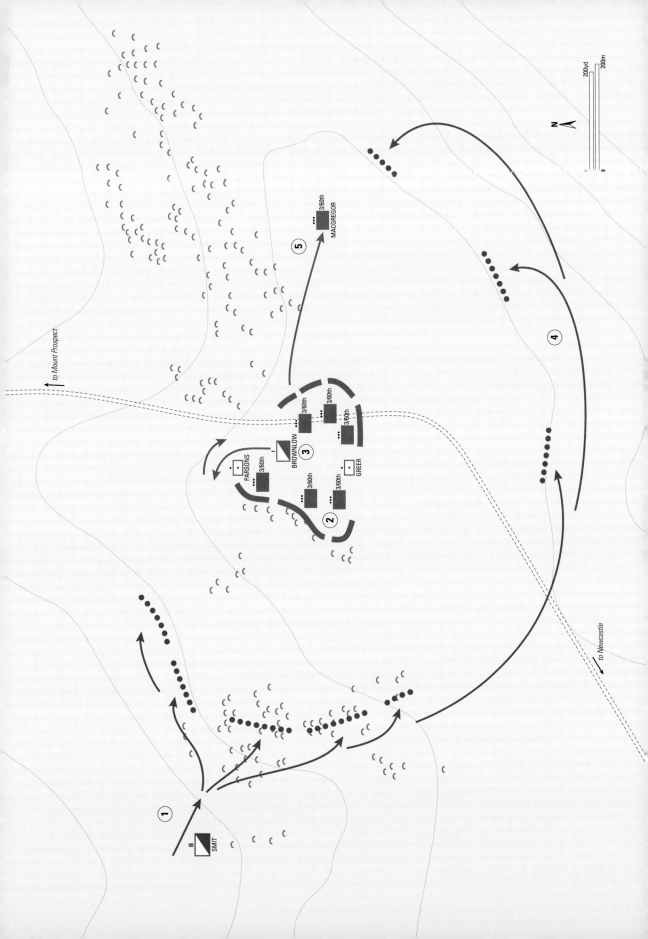

to Mount Prospect

to Newcastle

SMIT

1

2

3

BROWNLOW

PARSONS

3/60th

3/60th

3/60th

GREER

3/60th

3/60th

5

MACGREGOR

3/60th

4

N

200yd
200m

INTO COMBAT

The defeat at Laing's Nek was particularly shocking to the British since it challenged their perceptions of Boer military capabilities. Colley felt that he had little choice but to remain at Mount Prospect until British reinforcements, hurried to southern Africa after Bronkhorstspruit, reached him. The Boers anticipated their arrival, however, and attempted to disrupt Colley's lines of communication to delay their arrival. In particular the road from Mount Prospect back down to Newcastle was vulnerable to attacks by Boer mounted patrols and Colley had too few mounted troops of his own to prevent them.

On 5 February Field Commandant-General Nicolaas Smit, a dynamic veteran of the Republic's 1876 war against the Pedi people, led some 200 men out of the Boer laagers to deny Colley use of the road. Smit's men swung wide of Colley's camp and, operating from a bivouac in the spurs of the uKhahlamba mountains, interrupted Colley's lines of communication and supply. After several days of this Colley decided to act. It was obvious work for cavalry troops but Colley had none available beyond the survivors of the Mounted Squadron, and instead he decided on a demonstration with a much larger force. Rather than entrust command to a subordinate, he set out from Mount Prospect himself at 0830hrs on 8 February at the head of five companies of the 3/60th Rifles, two 7-pdr and two 9-pdr guns, and 44 officers and men of the Mounted Squadron. The Mounted Squadron was again led by Brownlow, and seems to have been short of horses, taking just 38 with them. As Colley expected to be back by nightfall, no extra supplies of food or water were taken. A few miles down the track Colley approached the Ingogo River and left his two 7-pdrs and a company of the 3/60th Rifles to guard the crossing before pressing up the slope on the opposite bank and emerging on to a low plateau known as Schuinshoogte. As he arrived his forward scouts immediately returned to report that there were Boers ahead. A civilian war correspondent, Thomas Carter, rode forward to see for himself and spotted 'standing on a rise below our level, not more than 1000 yards away on the right, about a hundred Boers mounted. Our sudden appearance seemed to startle and confuse them, as they reined up suddenly, and waited a minute or two, as if hesitating what to do' (Carter 1900: 199).

Smit had been present at Bronkhorstspruit and it was his intention to repeat similar tactics here. Despite the fact that he had failed to take Colley by surprise, his reaction now would not only secure the initiative for the Boers, but also set a tactical precedent in the struggles to come. According to Carter,

> There they stood, a splendid mark for our guns. Instantly the order was given to prepare for action; the artillery horses swung round at the double-quick, and one gun was loaded and rapidly trained. The Boers in sight appeared to hardly comprehend the movement until our gunners were on the point of firing; then they wheeled round and galloped for the bottom of the donga or ravine which separated them from us, taking an oblique course to break the steepness of the descent. As they ran, shell number one went whizzing over their heads, and burst far away beyond them. (Carter 1900: 199)

Yet Carter had missed the point of the Boer manoeuvre – instead of running to dodge the shells, Smit had attacked. As his men reached the hollows at the foot of the Schuinshoogte plateau they dismounted and, leaving their horses to look after themselves, began to skirmish forward up the slopes towards the British position. As they did so, Colley deployed his men in an extended horseshoe line around the broken edge of the plateau where a line of boulders afforded some cover. On top of the rise the grass was short but it grew longer on the slopes beyond, obscuring patches of boulders that were scattered among it here and there, and this gave the Boers the advantage, as Carter noticed:

> It soon became apparent that left, right, front and rear, we were completely
> surrounded by the enemy, who kept under cover, taking advantage of the long
> grass and boulders so well that it was a difficult thing to spy a Boer. Our men were
> all lying down behind rocks and stones, and firing only when they saw a head or
> an arm of an opponent. (Carter 1900: 200)

It was a type of warfare at which the Boers excelled, choosing individual targets and advancing at their own pace, and the British were further hampered by being silhouetted against the skyline above. The summit of the rise was largely safe from Boer fire – because they were shooting upwards, most of it passed high and away from the edges – but any British soldier who exposed himself on the perimeter immediately attracted fire. Those on horseback were particularly vulnerable as the Boers picked off both mounted officers and gun-teams. Worst of all, the crews of the two 9-pdrs were hopelessly exposed:

> The artillerymen suffered the heaviest because they had no cover except behind the
> guns, and that was miserable shelter, seeing the determination with which the enemy
> shot from close quarters incessantly at the gunners. Captain [C.R.] Greer, who was
> directing the fire on the southern edge of the plateau, was killed very early in the day.
> Taking the fuse from the hand of one of his men, who was not moving as smartly as
> his commander wished, he was on the point of inserting it in the vent when a bullet,
> glancing off the broad arrow of the gun, killed him immediately. (Carter 1900: 202)

It was in an attempt to ease the pressure on the gunners that Colley then directed his mounted men to try to sweep around the opposite Boer flank. It was an ambitious move and totally unsuited to the small number of men

During the First Anglo-Boer War, British garrisons within the territory were besieged by the Boers; these are Boer prisoners captured in skirmishes outside Pretoria. They have been disarmed, but their appearance is otherwise typical of the fashions among farmers in the 1880s.

Major Brownlow's sortie

This scene shows the height of the battle of Ingogo (Schuinshoogte) at about 1300hrs on 8 February 1881. To break the stalemate Colley directed Brownlow's Mounted Squadron to charge out on his flank in an attempt to prevent the Boers from encircling him completely. Advancing past the British line, the Mounted Squadron moved to the open ground beyond, where they attempted to deploy to charge. They were now exposed to the fire of Boers sheltering behind rocks only 160yd away down the slope, however, and attracted a hail of bullets. The Boers seem to have aimed particularly at the horses and within a very short space of time the majority of them were hit, although only one man was wounded. Brownlow's force was effectively destroyed before the charge had even begun, and he was forced to withdraw his men back to the centre of the plateau.

A vedette of the 1st (King's) Dragoon Guards skirmishing with a Boer outpost in 1881. The Natal Field Force was chronically short of cavalry, and the Mounted Squadron was cobbled together from a core of personnel of the 1st (King's) Dragoon Guards and mounted infantry.

under Brownlow's command, most of whom were not trained in cavalry tactics. The incident was over very quickly, and amid all the carnage taking place on the Schuinshoogte plateau its significance was almost lost; yet, taken together with the disastrous charge at Laing's Nek, Brownlow's second sortie confirmed the fatal obsolescence of conventional British cavalry tactics in the face of Boer firepower.

After Brownlow's repulse the Boers began to extend their position to surround the British entirely. At about 1500hrs Colley – who had moved coolly about the summit, ignoring the bullets singing past him – saw the danger and ordered half of I Company of the 3/60th Rifles led by one of his staff, Captain J.C. MacGregor, to sally out to prevent the movement. The slope was less steep on this side and Colley intended that MacGregor should push forward just enough to check the Boer encirclement, but MacGregor misjudged the situation and led his men to a point 600yd away from the main British position. They were now exposed to Boer fire all the way – MacGregor himself, leading on horseback, was soon shot – and when they arrived the men found only a clump of low boulders behind which to shelter. The nearest Boers were only 50yd away and afterwards Carter noted that 'every stone that partially concealed either a Boer or a man of the 60th [was] literally whitened over with the splash of lead … the bullets had simply hailed' (Carter 1900: 204).

Of the party who set out with MacGregor, 56 were killed or wounded and only four riflemen and one officer survived, but the move did prevent Smit's men from completing their encirclement. Around the summit of the high ground, however, the British position was becoming serious. The men had now been lying behind boulders for hours engaging in a protracted firefight which the Boers were undoubtedly winning. Carter noted that one man, 'shooting from a stone, had to change his position. In doing so his foot was caught in a crevice, and in endeavouring to extricate himself he exposed his body to the enemy. Before he could get his foot loose he was shot twice' (Carter 1900: 219). After the battle, Carter examined British helmets abandoned on the ground and noticed that 'In one I found six bullet-holes, five in the upper part – they must have passed clear of the wearer's head – the sixth had torn away the side of the helmet where the band runs, and without doubt was a fatal wound. Amongst other helmets lying there were several which had two or three bullet holes in them' (Carter 1900: 224).

Most of the gunners were down, British casualties were mounting, men were tired, hungry and thirsty and most of the horses had been either killed or wounded. Since Colley had brought no water supplies with him the men had exhausted the contents of their water-bottles and the wounded, in particular, were desperate. Late in the afternoon, to add to the miseries of both sides, a

An unidentified member of the 58th Regiment who served with Colley's Mounted Squadron and was perhaps a veteran of Laing's Nek and Ingogo. Like all mounted infantry at this period he is wearing the scarlet jacket (in this case the dress tunic) of his parent regiment and corduroy riding breeches. In the field his helmet would have been stripped of brass fittings and dulled with a stain made from tea or coffee. He is wearing his campaign medal for the earlier Anglo-Zulu War.

Nicolaas Jacobus Smit

Descended from some of the first Dutch Calvinist settlers at the Cape, the future commander of the Boer forces at Ingogo was born at Doornbos, near Graaff Reinet in the Eastern Cape, on 5 May 1837. In May 1876 he was appointed a lieutenant-general during the unsuccessful campaign against the Pedi kingdom, the failure of which was one of the justifications cited by the British for the annexation of the Transvaal. Nevertheless, Smit enjoyed a good military reputation and one British officer commented that he was 'one of the ablest leaders of mounted infantry that appeared in modern war', while Colley himself thought him 'an intelligent and fine man, courteous and humane in everything connected with the wounded, and gallant in action' (Butler 1899: 390 & 312).

When the old Transvaal flag, the *Vierkleur* (four colour), was raised by the Republicans in December 1880, Smit addressed the crowd, saying, 'This is the flag of our fathers, dear to them and double dear to us. Let us show that we wish to keep it and, if it is asked, that we give our blood for it' (quoted in Meintjes 1971: 67–68). When the Boers awoke in their laagers on 27 February to find that Colley had occupied the summit of Majuba, Smit was among those who organized the counter-attack, calling out, 'Those who are not cowards must follow us!' (quoted in Lehmann 1972: 241). Appointed Field Commandant-General at the outbreak of hostilities, Smit played a significant role in all the battles, and was present at Bronkhorstspruit, Laing's Nek, Ingogo and Majuba. Smit was also involved in the peace negotiations at the end of the First Anglo-Boer War.

During the 1890s Smit was made Vice-President of the Transvaal Republic, but he did not live to see the outbreak of the Second Anglo-Boer War, dying in Pretoria on 4 April 1896.

fierce thunderstorm broke overhead, drenching the combatants. Furthermore, the numbers of Boers engaged had actually increased as the sound of shooting had drawn more men from Joubert's camps beyond Laing's Nek, and by late afternoon there were perhaps 500 Boers taking part. Yet although the Boers had undoubtedly dominated the field with their fire, neither side was able to break the stalemate – having no training in hand-to-hand combat, the Boers hung back from making a final rush.

As evening fell, Colley realized that his men could not hope to spend the night where they were and defend themselves against a fresh attack in the morning. His only choice was either to surrender, or to try to slip away under cover of darkness. At about 2130hrs Colley ordered the surviving horses to be attached to the guns. There was little hope of moving the most badly wounded and they were left on the field in the care of a surgeon and a chaplain – the remainder of his command were formed into a hollow square and, at about 2330hrs, Colley abandoned the battlefield. A strict silence was observed, but the movement of so many men and gun carriages across the stony ground would have been obvious to any Boers watching; for once, though, Colley was lucky: Smit had been so convinced that the British were in no position to move from the heights that he had excused his men guard-duty that night to escape from the rain.

Colley's night march was a suitably grim end to a dreadful day for the British. When they reached the Ingogo River they found it swollen by the rain and chest-high, and several men were swept away and drowned. In the darkness there was no sign of the men left to guard the drifts, and as Colley's men pressed on the exhausted horses would only drag the limbers with the help of equally exhausted men. Colley finally returned to Mount Prospect just as dawn was breaking at 0400hrs on the morning of the 9th. When, at about the same time, Smit arrived at Schuinshoogte to resume the battle, he was amazed to find it deserted but for the dead and dying.

Joseph Venables enlisted in the 1st (King's) Dragoon Guards in the 1870s. Serving throughout the Anglo-Zulu War, Venables was one of those left behind in Natal when the rest of the regiment departed. As such he was one of the Dragoon Guards who formed the core of Colley's Mounted Squadron despatched to northern Natal. Ho wrote that 'the Boers are all good shots, they won't be like the Zulus, you will see we shall lose a good many men before it is settled' (quoted in Crouch & Knight 1981: 26).

Venables took part in the attack at Laing's Nek, where his horse was shot under him and he was knocked unconscious. After the battle some Boers found him and thought him dead – they found a letter in his pocket which he had written to his family but not posted; it was later passed on to them with a covering note from the Secretary for the South African Republic who regretted Venables' death as 'a victim of the mischievous policy of the English government – who send brave soldiers against men who only defend their liberty' (quoted in Crouch & Knight 1981: 27). In fact, Venables was not dead and was taken prisoner. During his time in captivity he was 'well treated, and received the same food as the people themselves' (Norris-Newman 1882: 151).

In April 1881 he was released into British care; he returned to the UK and recovered from his injuries, but considered that the Mounted Squadron had been badly handled during the war – 'The 600', he wrote, referring to the Light Brigade in the Crimea, 'never made so foolish a charge' (quoted in Crouch & Knight 1981: 28). He left the Army but volunteered for service again in 1914, raising a company of men from among the destitute in Liverpool. He died in 1933 aged 78.

Although Smit had missed a chance to destroy Colley's forces entirely, the battle had undoubtedly been a British defeat. Colley had failed in his objective to clear the road to Newcastle, and his losses were shocking. The 3/60th Rifles had lost two officers and 56 men killed and three officers and 60 men wounded – a casualty rate of 40 per cent of their men involved. The Royal Artillery had lost one officer and two men killed and 11 men wounded. Colley himself was unhurt but had lost two of his staff, while the Mounted Squadron had lost just three men killed and two wounded but had lost 23 of their 38 horses, destroying it as an effective unit. Boer losses were in the region of ten men killed or mortally wounded and seven wounded.

There was worse to come. News of this further defeat persuaded the Government in London to agree to an armistice to discuss the possibility of the annexation of the Transvaal being withdrawn. Colley, disappointed that this would deny him the opportunity to retrieve his honour in the field, moved to occupy Majuba Hill on the night of 26/27 February 1881. Almost certainly he regarded the occupation as little more than a bargaining ploy to apply pressure to the Boers since it overlooked the Boer positions; instead, on the morning of the 27th, the Boers mounted an attack to drive him off, skirmishing up the slope much as they had at Ingogo. Attacking in short rushes supported by covering fire the Boers overran the summit, driving the British off and killing Colley in the process.

The First Anglo-Boer War was the only war of the many during the Victorian era in which the British lost both every major battle and the subsequent peace. The return of the Transvaal Territory to the Boer Republic was agreed in late 1881, but the abandonment of English-speaking settlers and pro-British African groups to a hard-line Afrikaner government would create a legacy of bitterness, exacerbated by the discovery of gold in 1886 which attracted intense financial speculation and interest, mostly from British entrepreneurs.

Bothaville (Doornkraal)

6 November 1900

The conservative approach of British Regular cavalry at the beginning of the Second Anglo-Boer War, together with their unfamiliarity with the landscape, left them vulnerable to more fluid Boer attacks; here, a vedette is surprised outside Ladysmith. While the Boer commando system had remained essentially unchanged since 1881, the British Army had changed significantly. As early as 1881 troops sent to reinforce Colley from India were wearing khaki field uniforms and by 1899 this was universal among all arms. The single-shot Martini-Henry rifle had given way to the magazine Lee-Metford and its later variant, the Lee-Enfield. Although British tactical doctrine continued to favour mass attacks and volley-firing, there was a growing realization that extended formations and greater flexibility were an essential requirement of warfare against an opponent armed with accurate, long-range, rapid-firing small arms.

BACKGROUND TO BATTLE

After decades of escalating tension, the Second Anglo-Boer War broke out on 11 October 1899 when Boer forces invaded British territory in the Cape and Natal colonies. Although British intelligence estimates placed the total number of Boers under arms at 90,000 men, it is unlikely that more than 40,000 Boers were in the field at any given time. Britain had scarcely 10,000 men in southern Africa when the war broke out, and so an army corps – 47,000 men, including seven cavalry regiments – was mobilized in the UK. While this was assembling some 10,000 troops were sent from India as interim reinforcements.

Boer forces, taking advantage of their superior numbers and the early overconfidence of British commanders, were able to press into northern Natal and the Cape Colony, and to threaten the strategic town of Mafikeng. In northern Natal Commandant-General Piet Joubert trapped Lieutenant-General Sir George Stuart White – who had recently arrived with reinforcements intended to hold Natal until a full British mobilization took place – in the garrison-town of Ladysmith. Free State commandos also surrounded the diamond town of Kimberley in the northern Cape. If the Boers had hoped that by applying pressure they would force the British to negotiate – as they had after Majuba Hill – they were mistaken, and with the arrival of the 1st Army Corps in late 1899 the British went on the offensive to relieve the besieged towns. There was heavy fighting on the Ladysmith and Kimberley fronts as the British tried unsuccessfully to fight their way through the Boer cordons at Colenso and Spioenkop and Modder River and Magersfontein respectively. These battles largely followed the pattern of Laing's Nek, with the Boers concealed behind defensive features and the British mounting unsuccessful assaults.

In this, the so-called conventional phase of the war, the Boers exploited their advantage in defence rather than mobility and the battles were, despite occasional mounted forays on both sides, essentially infantry affairs. Although Ladysmith was relieved largely through successful infantry action, under artillery support, in the actions along the Thukela Heights in February 1900, a brigade of Regular cavalry under Lieutenant-General Sir John French made a wide flanking march which largely persuaded the Boers to abandon their positions around Kimberley. French's outflanking of the Boer positions led the Boer commandant on the Kimberley front, Piet Cronjé, to retreat towards the Free State capital of Bloemfontein. Cronjé refused to abandon his wagon-train and artillery, however, and he was caught at Paardeberg on the banks of the Modder River on 18 February 1900. Here he constructed a wagon-laager in traditional style on the banks of the river and was subjected to a series of British attacks until he finally agreed to surrender with over 4,000 men on 27 February – the anniversary of Majuba Hill.

A charge by Lancers from the Boer perspective, loosely based on the charge of the 5th Lancers at Elandslaagte. In fact this picture is largely propaganda – despite the occasional success, British Regular cavalry were seldom able to employ the *arme blanche* in action against the Boers because the nature of the fighting made charges to contact extremely costly. At the first battle of the war, Talana (20 October 1899), the Boers occupied a hill overlooking the town of Dundee; they were driven off by a costly frontal attack by British infantry, but when a squadron of the 18th Hussars attempted to encircle the hill to cut off the retreating Boers, in classic cavalry style, they became separated from the main force in a heavy mist and blundered into fresh Boer troops who forced them to surrender. In contrast, at Elandslaagte, the following day, two squadrons from the 5th (Royal Irish) Lancers and 5th (Princess Charlotte of Wales's) Dragoon Guards successfully charged retreating Boers at the end of the action, causing heavy casualties.

The dash by Lieutenant-General Sir John French's Regular cavalry brigade to relieve Kimberley. French's long sweep around the Boer flank was a decisive factor in the relief, but largely exhausted his horses, however, putting as many as 3,500 out of action out of an initial force of 5,000, with consequences that would affect the performance of the Regular cavalry throughout the war. Generally, in the early part of the war, conventional cavalry *arme blanche* tactics proved too costly to be practicable, British horses did not always cope well in southern African conditions, cavalry scouting was often ineffective and the reluctance of the Regular cavalry at this stage to fight on foot hampered their tactical usefulness. Even before the end of the conventional phase the British turned increasingly to either Regular mounted-infantry units or to locally raised units who fought in the same manner.

With both Kimberley and Ladysmith relieved the British were able to advance and capture the capitals of the Boer republics, Bloemfontein on 13 March and Pretoria on 5 June, but while some Boers were prepared to surrender, others were determined to continue fighting. With many of the older, more conservative commandants such as Cronjé in captivity a number of younger, more dynamic commandants rose to authority and the large Boer concentrations which had characterized the outbreak of the war gave way to smaller, more streamlined, mobile and determined forces. Although the Boers never entirely abandoned their reliance on wheeled transport they did abandon the long cumbersome wagon-trains of the early war and the fighting entered a new phase – one in which the Boers functioned as highly mobile guerrilla units which avoided the main British concentrations but struck instead at supply trains and railway lines. In response the British, too, were forced to change their methods, shifting away from conventional tactics and relying on more mobile flying columns. Regular cavalry were expected to function increasingly as mounted infantry, and they were supported by much greater numbers of Regular mounted-infantry, Yeomanry and Colonial Volunteer units, all of whom fought in a mounted-infantry manner.

From late 1900 to 1902, the war became a struggle in which mounted men who fought on foot dominated the battlefield on both sides. In July 1900 the President of the Free State, Marthinus Theunis Steyn, and most of the surviving Free State commandos regrouped in a large natural amphitheatre surrounded by mountains known as the Brandwater Basin. The British had successfully surrounded the basin, however, and it was decided that Steyn should escape, accompanied by General Christiaan Rudolf de Wet and his commandos. De Wet was a farmer in his mid-forties who had been part of the Heilbron commando at the beginning of the war; he had taken part in the fighting in Natal and had distinguished himself to the extent that Steyn had made him a general and, after the surrender at Paardeberg, commandant-in-chief of the Free State forces. De Wet had already proved himself adept at the evolving style of guerrilla warfare, and won a daring victory over the British at Sanna's Post near Bloemfontein in March and another at Roodewal in June. This latter victory had encouraged the British to adopt stricter counter-insurgency measures, including the burning of Boer farms. On the night of 15 July, however, Steyn and De Wet slipped through the passes in the nick of time – on 30 July the Boers surrendered. Over 4,000 men were captured in the biggest British success since Paardeberg.

Ranging across the Free State with the British in pursuit, De Wet joined an unsuccessful attack on a British position at Fredrikstad in late October. On the 27th, Australian troops and British mounted infantry almost caught De Wet crossing the Vaal River, but he managed to slip away under the cover of a thunderstorm. At the beginning of November, however, De Wet met with President Steyn and the commando of about 800 men camped on a farm called Doornkraal a few miles south of the village of Bothaville. During the course of this meeting Steyn and De Wet agreed that in order to invigorate the Boer cause in the Free State, De Wet should make a foray into the Cape Colony to rally Boer rebels there.

In the meantime, British mounted troops under the command of Major-General Charles Knox had been sweeping westwards trying to pick up De Wet's trail. On 5 November Lieutenant-Colonel Philip Le Gallais occupied Bothaville with a column consisting of the 5th, 7th and 8th Mounted Infantry, the 17th and 18th companies of Imperial Yeomanry and four guns of U Battery, Royal Horse Artillery. The village had been destroyed during British sweeps earlier in the year, but as they occupied the ruins Le Gallais' men came under fire from Boer guns on the Valsch (Vals) River nearby. At the same time Knox was about 6 miles away with a body of troops commanded by Captain Henry de Beauvoir De Lisle. Le Gallais allowed his men a few hours' sleep before mounting up at 0400hrs on 6 November to investigate the Boer presence.

The interior of General Piet Cronjé's wagon-laager after the Boer defeat at Paardeberg. Cronjé's retreat from the Kimberley lines was hampered by his wagon-train, allowing the British to intercept him, and the vulnerability of his subsequent laager to artillery and small-arms fire spelled the end of the Boers' defensive reliance on the wagon. Cronjé's defeat proved that tactics which had been successful against generations of African enemies were now entirely inappropriate, but by forcing the Boers to give up their dependence on long wagon-trains it freed the commandos to play to their other strengths – their knowledge of the country and their mobility. During the guerrilla war the commandos would retain only limited wheeled transport and on longer raids did without it altogether.

MAP KEY

1 Night of 5/6 November: Having slipped through pursuing British columns near the town of Rothaville, General Christiaan Rudolf de Wet and his men cross the Valsch (Vals) River and laager on the Doornkraal farm.

2 c.0530hrs: Having surprised a Boer picquet at the river, a detachment of 60 men of the 5th Mounted Infantry under Major Kenneth Lean, arrive at this low ridge. Lean realizes he has surprised the Boers and immediately opens fire.

3 c.0540hrs: As Lean opens fire another small detachment of the 5th Mounted Infantry arrives at the small cluster of buildings which constitute the Doornkraal farmhouse – the 'Red House', another neighbouring house and a small cattle-kraal. A small group under Captain Colville occupies the cattle-kraal while another group under Lieutenant Percy Smith occupies the buildings.

4 c.0545hrs: The Boers are caught by surprise. The President of the Free State, Marthinus Steyn, is hurried away to safety, and many of the Boers mount their horses and flee, despite efforts by De Wet to rally them. A number of Boers who are not able to escape occupy the orchard and, sheltering behind the forward walls, return fire.

5 c.0600hrs: The commander of the British column, Lieutenant-Colonel Philip Le Gallais, arrives on the battlefield and hurries to the most forward point on the British line, the Red House. From here he attempts to direct the battle – but the Red House is dangerously exposed to Boer fire from the right of the walled orchard, and Le Gallais is fatally wounded by shots passing through the open door.

6 c.0615hrs: Having managed to occupy a small pigsty lying between the orchard and the ridge occupied by the British amid the confusion of the British arrival, three Boers begin to pick off a number of Major Lean's men, firing from behind the rocks on the summit of the ridge. They occupy this vantage point for up to two hours before suffering a direct hit from the British artillery.

7 c.0615hrs: Two guns of U Battery, Royal Horse Artillery, commanded by Lieutenant Otter Barry, arrive to support the 5th Mounted Infantry and deploy on their right flank, drawing heavy Boer fire.

8 c.0630hrs: In response to De Wet's efforts some of the Boers who had fled at the beginning of the action now begin to reappear on the battlefield, advancing to the right of the dam and threatening the farm buildings and the British left.

9 c.0700hrs: Further British reinforcements – 8th Mounted Infantry and a further gun of U Battery commanded by Captain Mair – shore up the British left. They push forward to challenge the new advance of the Boer right. A firefight ensues.

10 c.0730hrs: A small detachment of the 17th and 18th companies, Imperial Yeomanry arrives on the battlefield and deploys on the British right. They are supported later (about 0900hrs) by a detachment of the Western Australian Mounted Infantry from Major-General Charles Knox's column.

11 c.0800hrs: Detachments of the 7th Mounted Infantry – under Major Welsh – arrive on the British left. They are reinforced by the remainder of the 7th Mounted Infantry, a pom-pom and a detachment of the New South Wales Mounted Rifles led by Captain Henry de Beauvoir De Lisle of Knox's column. De Lisle mounts an attack on the Boer right, driving it back beyond the cover of a small white farm outbuilding.

12 c.0930hrs: With the arrival of British reinforcements, Major Lean directs his men of the 5th Mounted Infantry to charge towards the Boer position in the orchard. He is supported by the Western Australian Mounted Infantry on his right; the Imperial Yeomanry detachment move around to their right to encircle the Boer left.

13 c.0930hrs: Seeing the 5th Mounted Infantry charging towards them, and unable to escape, the Boers surrender.

14 c.0930hrs: Major Welsh's detachments of the 7th and 8th Mounted Infantry arrive in the Boer rear at about the time the Boers in the orchard surrender. The battle is over.

Battlefield environment

The terrain of Bothaville is largely flat, the original farmhouse standing in typical isolation on the veldt surrounded by a cluster of outbuildings. The dam – where a shallow stream had been blocked off to provide a water-hole for cattle – was no more than a few feet deep. Even the rises which masked the British approach, and which were occupied by British mounted infantry at the start of the battle, are only a few feet high, just sufficient to offer some protection to horses sheltered behind them. Only the dry-stone wall surrounding the farm orchard and gardens, and which abutted the dam wall to take advantage of the drainage,

provided a significant feature for defence. The walled orchard proved something of a mixed blessing, for while it afforded protection against British rifle-fire and a clear line of sight into the farm buildings it offered little shelter against artillery fire and no escape route, and the defenders were effectively trapped. Nevertheless, it is significant that away from the tussle for the farm itself, both sides used the open country to good effect for mounted men – De Wet was able to muster some of his fleeing men and try to counter-attack while the British, as fresh troops arrived, were able to try to outflank the Boers in return.

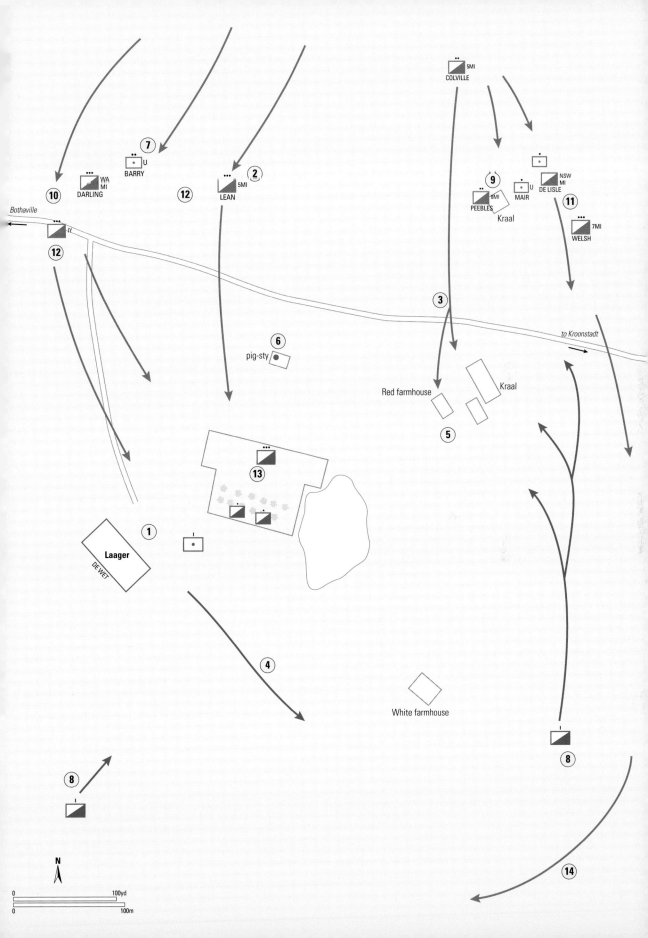

COLVILLE ·· 5MI

⑦
BARRY ·· U

WA
DARLING ··· MI

⑩

⑫

LEAN ··· 5MI
②

⑨ ·

PEEBLES ·· 8MI

MAIR · U

DE LISLE · NSW MI

⑪

WELSH ··· 7MI

Kraal

Bothaville
···Y

⑫

③

to Kroonstadt

pig-sty ⑥

Red farmhouse

Kraal

⑤

⑬ ···

⑧

① **Laager**
DE WET

·

④

White farmhouse

⑧ ·

⑧ ·

⑭

N

0   100yd
0   100m

INTO COMBAT

De Wet and Steyn were encamped that night at Doornkraal, about 7 miles from Bothaville on the other side of the Valsch. The countryside was typical of the wide-open expanses of the Free State, and the commando had established a laager close to two ruined buildings which constituted the farm. The farmer had blocked a wet hollow near the buildings to produce a pool of water where the Boers had watered their horses and oxen. Near the buildings was a stone enclosure filled with fruit trees. De Wet, who was aware of the proximity of the pursuing British, nevertheless felt secure with the river between them and spent the night 'without suspecting any harm':

> I placed an outpost that night close to the river and told them to stay there until the following day. The burghers of this watch returned in the morning and reported that they had seen nothing but wreaths of smoke ascending from the north bank of the river. They believed that these came from the English camp.
>
> We were still safe then – or so we believed. (De Wet 1902: 185)

In fact, early on the morning of the 6th a detachment from Le Gallais' column, some 67 men of the 5th Mounted Infantry under Major Kenneth Lean, scouting out towards Doornkraal, had stumbled across one of De Wet's picquets of five men, all asleep. The Boers were captured without a shot being fired and Lean could plainly see the tracks of De Wet's guns leading away from the river. Lean at once sent back for Le Gallais' guns and pressed on himself. He had not gone far before he crested a low rise and saw the Boer encampment at Doornkraal scarcely more than 300yd ahead. There was very little sign of activity and, considering the proximity of the two armies, it seemed unusually quiet; the oxen were outspanned and horses were grazing about, and there seemed no more obvious picquets. It was now 0530hrs, and Lean decided to attack.

In the camp De Wet had just taken the report from his outpost, who had declared all was quiet, when

> … the corporal who had brought this report had but just left me, and was scarcely 100 paces off when I heard the report of rifles. I thought at first that it was only some cattle being shot for food, but all at once there were more shots, and what did we see? The English were within three hundred paces of us, on a little hill near Bothaville, and close to the spot from whence my outpost had just returned.
>
> It was early morning. The sun had not risen more than twenty minutes and many of the burghers still lay asleep in their blankets. (De Wet 1902: 185–86)

For once, it was De Wet who had been caught napping:

> The scene which ensued was unlike anything I had ever witnessed before. I heard a good deal about panics – I was now to see one with my own eyes. Whilst I was looking for my horse to get him up-saddled a few of the burghers were making some sort of stand against the enemy. But all those who had already up-saddled were riding away at breakneck speed. Many even were leaving their saddles behind and galloping off bare-back. As I up-saddled my horse I called out to them –

'Don't run away! Come back and storm the enemy's position!' But it was no use – a panic had seized them, and the victims of that panic were those brave men who had never thought of flight, but only of resisting the enemy! (De Wet 1902: 186)

As those men who had managed to saddle their horses rode from the field as fast as they could De Wet intercepted one after another, but to no avail, 'for as I stopped them at one point others galloped past me, and I was thus kept dodging from point to point, until the whole commando was out of range of the firing' (De Wet 1902: 186). Among those who got safely away was President Steyn. Aware of the loss to the Boer cause if Steyn were killed or captured his adjutant, Du Preez, had kept the President's horse saddled and tied to a supply wagon. While Du Preez hurried off to try to delay the British advance, Steyn mounted his horse and rode away.

In the meantime, about 130 burghers who had not managed to get away had taken what cover they could around the farm buildings. Most had occupied the orchard and, nestled down behind the stone walls, had opened a heavy fire on Lean's men on the ridge in front of them. The right-hand edge of the orchard lay close to the farm buildings and some Boers had managed to find shelter around the nearer of two buildings but the further, made of red brick, lay closest to the British positions. Out in front of the orchard, much closer to Lean's line, was a small pigsty which just three brave burghers had occupied.

At the same time some of Lean's men made for the red farmhouse. A Captain Colville led a small detachment of the 5th Mounted Infantry into another outlying stone kraal beside the building while Lieutenant Percy Smith and a handful of men managed to enter the building. They had just done so when a two-gun section of U Battery, Royal Horse Artillery, under Lieutenant Otter Barry arrived, but as the gunners came over the rise next to Lean's men their lead horses were shot by the Boer snipers in the pigsty. With no option but to stay where they were, Barry's guns came into action on the spot although the crews, too, soon began to take casualties. By this stage, however, the rest of Le Gallais' command was coming up quickly and detachments of the 8th Mounted Infantry and two more guns from U Battery deployed on Lean's left while a small party of the Imperial Yeomanry took up a position to the right.

When Le Gallais himself arrived he went immediately to the red farmhouse. From here he could see that, in the distance, De Wet's attempts to rally the fleeing burghers seemed to be having some effect as a number were returning to the battlefield, and moving towards the buildings to support the Boer right. He ordered that troops guarding his baggage to the rear be hurried up to reinforce the left and sent a message back to Knox asking for his support, but as the volume of close-range rifle-fire grew British casualties around the farmhouse began to mount. As usual, the Boers targeted the British officers, who could be seen clearly at ranges of only 140yd. Captain Colville, in the kraal near the buildings, was wounded, and a Captain Engelbach killed nearby. The two guns of U Battery also suffered and were put out of action, but it was the red farmhouse that attracted most Boer fire.

Here, two doors on opposite walls and opening to the outside were open, and any officer who passed between them within the building was silhouetted against the light to the burghers defending the orchard wall. Le Gallais himself stepped across the gap and was shot through the left side of the chest and his second-in-command, Lieutenant-Colonel Walter Ross, was hit twice a few minutes later. Some of the Boers were firing bullets with the points filed off, which meant that they almost exploded on impact; the resulting wounds were horrific. One bullet struck Ross on the point of his lower jaw and shattered it – he survived, but his jaw was later amputated (he lived on soup and milk for some time, but later found that he could eat mince; he survived to command a brigade in World War I). Captain Williams, Ross' staff officer, was hit no fewer than six times and killed, and Lieutenant Smith and several of his men were wounded.

For two hours the battle raged as a desperate close-range firefight. The gunners of U Battery had been lobbing shells into the laager behind the Boer positions, and were close enough to fire occasional rounds of case-shot against the walls in front of them. Eventually, their fire had its effect – a shell bursting in the white farmhouse killed four Boers sheltering there, while another finally obliterated the Boer marksmen in the pigsty between the lines.

The longer the battle went on the closer came the British reinforcements. Major-General Knox had broken his camp at 0500hrs and begun moving towards Bothaville. Shortly afterwards he heard the sound of Le Gallais' guns, and ordered De Lisle's men forward at full speed. De Lisle arrived on the battlefield about 0900hrs and immediately took charge of the action. He went forward to the red farmhouse and saw for himself the carnage there – the floor was littered with dead and badly injured men, the walls and floor were spattered with blood – and promptly ordered his own men to reinforce the British left in an attempt to drive back the Boer counter-attack. A pom-

pom (quick-firing Maxim-Nordenfelt 1-pdr) and one of U Battery's guns were brought forward to shell the white farmhouse while Major Welsh was ordered to gather elements of the 7th and 8th Mounted Infantry to try to work around the extreme Boer right with the intention eventually of taking those placed in the orchard in the rear. As more men of De Lisle's command arrived – Kitchener's Horse, the Western Australian Mounted Infantry and 6th Mounted Infantry – they were sent to reinforce Lean's centre and right. Finally, at about 0930hrs, the last of De Lisle's men arrived. On the left Welsh had been mortally wounded and his second-in-command killed, but the turning movement was gaining ground and the Boers in the orchard were increasingly isolated and coming under fire from various points of the field. De Lisle realized that the battle had reached its critical moment, and he ordered Major Lean to gather a storming party from the 5th Mounted Infantry and 80 Western Australians under Lieutenant Darling. The party fixed bayonets and rushed forward in open order against the Boers still sheltering behind the stone wall. The sight of the sun glinting on the bayonets was too much for the Boers, who as civilians had never trained in close-quarter fighting techniques; before the rush struck home they held up a white flag and stood with their hands up.

As the British rounded up the prisoners, feelings ran high against them for their use of 'explosive' bullets. These were banned by the Hague Convention, but the Boer republics were not signatories to the terms – nevertheless, the

British Regular mounted infantry defend the rise against hot Boer fire from the walled orchard at Bothaville.

Rushing the orchard

Boer view: The Boers generally preferred to fight dispersed among the protection of natural features, but at Bothaville the speed of the unexpected British attack had forced the Boers to take shelter in the walled orchard. This at least provided some cover and commanded open ground towards the British position, while the right of the orchard looked towards the 'Red House' and farm buildings which Le Gallais and his staff had occupied. Le Gallais had tried to press an attack from this position, but it was too exposed to accurate Boer return fire, and indeed Le Gallais and several of his officers were killed or wounded inside the buildings themselves. The Boers were also able to pick off the gun-crews of the British artillery as it arrived and deployed for action. Even so, British return fire caused casualties at the orchard wall and, without their horses, the Boers were largely trapped, unable to escape or even move to a different position without breaking cover. The fighting had been going on for about four hours when, taking advantage of the arrival of reinforcements, Major Lean launched his charge; here the British, with bayonets fixed, are beginning to rush forward across the intervening ground. With no line of retreat, and with no tradition or training in close-quarter combat, the Boers in the orchard will raise a white flag and surrender before the charge strikes home.

British view: The climax of the battle of Bothaville at about 0945hrs on 6 November 1900. De Wet's forces, attempting to avoid two British mounted columns pursuing them, had passed the town of Bothaville and bivouacked on the Doornkraal farm a few miles away. The terrain was typically open Free State grasslands and the farm consisted of a small cluster of buildings, a walled orchard and a dammed water-hole. De Wet had camped in a traditional laager close to the farm buildings. At 0500hrs, Lean's detachment of the 5th Mounted Infantry had surprised a sleeping Boer picquet, occupied a rise looking across to the Boer camp and opened fire; many of the Boers fled while others, unable to reach their horses, sheltered behind the stone wall around the orchard and returned fire.

The British had occupied the farmhouses on their left, but here Le Gallais and several of his officers were shot through the open doors by Boers sheltering around the orchard. By 0700hrs however, troops from Knox's column began to reinforce the position and at about 0945hrs Major Lean assembled a storming party of men of the 5th Mounted Infantry, supported on his right by men of the Western Australian Mounted Infantry, who all fixed bayonets and rushed forward in open order from the cover of the ridge across the open ground towards the walled orchard. The view shows the farm buildings on the left where Le Gallais was mortally wounded, the orchard centre, and beyond to the right De Wet's artillery park and wagon-laager.

British considered the use of them a war crime and according to Le Gallais' staff officer, Major Hickie,

> I had all the prisoners searched for explosive bullets and found 2 with them in their pockets. These I ordered to be shot in half an hour. Unfortunately I met the General [Knox] and told him – he said 'All right, I leave it to you.' Ten minutes afterwards he sent to me that he would have them tried first. Result that now we have cooled down, we won't shoot a man in cold blood. (Quoted in Pakenham 1979: 476)

The British had captured most of De Wet's transport and artillery: three 75mm Krupp guns, one 1-pdr Krupp gun, one pom-pom, a Maxim and two guns De Wet had himself captured from the British, a 15-pdr from Colenso and a 12-pdr from Sanna's Post. Boer casualties were surprisingly light and reflected their good use of cover – just 17 men killed and a further 17 wounded. More damagingly, however, 97 unwounded men had been taken prisoner. British losses amounted to 33 killed and wounded, among them ten officers – a high proportion which reflected the way the Boers had been able to single them out as targets.

Though the battle of Bothaville was undoubtedly a British victory, the long-term advantages were soon squandered. Major-General Knox was reluctant to pursue the Boers immediately and De Wet escaped; freed from most of his baggage, he was now more mobile than ever, and within a fortnight was once again attacking British outposts.

ABOVE LEFT
The death of Lieutenant-Colonel Philip Le Gallais at the battle of Bothaville.

ABOVE RIGHT
Le Gallais in the dress uniform of the 8th (The King's Royal Irish) Hussars. Le Gallais proved himself an excellent exponent of mounted-infantry tactics, and Bothaville would prove one of the most successful actions of its type in the war. In contrast to the fumbling attacks of the First Anglo-Boer War or even the more risky formal cavalry tactics of the early part of the present conflict, Le Gallais had used his men's mobility to good effect, approaching the Boer camp so quickly and quietly that they had caught even De Wet off-guard, yet in the ensuing fighting they had skirmished well on foot. The final charge had been well timed and so effective that the Boers had not opposed it.

Modderfontein (Elands River)

17 September 1901

BACKGROUND TO BATTLE

By the beginning of 1901 the large concentrations of Boer troops which had characterized the early part of the war had gone, increasingly replaced by streamlined fighting groups, often of no more than a few hundred men, their original commando affiliations increasingly blurred. Some were still accompanied by the odd field gun or Maxim, although as mobility came to be recognized as a greater asset than firepower these were often abandoned together with all but the lightest carts. Relieved of the need to defend strategic objectives, the Boers ranged across the veldt, sometimes coming together to develop coordinated strategies, at other times dispersing and acting entirely independently, but always with the intention simply of prolonging the war and damaging the British where they could.

At first the British struggled to contain them. The conventional balance of troop types with which they had begun the war required a heavy logistical network to support them, and the slow-moving infantry columns with their great trains of ox-wagons were not only hopelessly cumbersome but were often themselves vulnerable to Boer guerrilla attacks. Instead, the British gradually changed emphasis, relegating the infantry to a supporting role and developing more rapid columns composed of mounted troops and light artillery. This change marked the emergence of mounted-infantry-style troops as the defining troop-type of the later war, but it was not achieved without cost as men were often required to learn their craft in the field, and the huge distances involved resulted in the loss of thousands of horses through exhaustion and overwork.

To reduce the mobility of the Boer commandos further the British began to tie up the landscape by means of chains of small improvised forts – blockhouses – linked by barbed-wire fences. Initially, these were constructed to protect the

railway lines – which the British used to transport men and supplies, and which were otherwise vulnerable to Boer attacks – but from July 1901 they began to extend them, too, across the open countryside, dividing up the veldt into sectors which could then be swept clear of Boer combatants with mounted columns. To deny the commandos the advantage of a civilian support base, Boer farms in those areas in the Free State and Transvaal where the commandos operated were destroyed and Boer non-combatants were removed to camps.

These strategies undoubtedly achieved some success, hampering the free movement of the commandos, reducing their supplies and gradually whittling away their numbers, but they had, by September 1901, made little appreciable impact on the Boer will to resist. Indeed, even the most carefully co-ordinated British sweeps were often hampered by a poor knowledge of the terrain while the Boers possessed a dash born of desperation. Many operations ended with Boer commandos slipping through gaps in the British cordon across terrain which had seemed impassable.

Nevertheless, this war of attrition took its toll. Those Boers who still carried their Mausers were often critically short of ammunition and many instead had resorted to using captured British Lee-Enfields. The clothing with which the burghers had taken to the field in October 1899 was long since worn out. One young Boer, Deneys Reitz – who left one of the best accounts of the war from the Boer perspective – recalled that 'My own wardrobe was typical; a ragged coat and worn trousers full of holes, with no shirt or underwear of any kind. On my feet were dilapidated rawhide sandals, patched and re-patched during eight months of wear, and I had only one frayed blanket to sleep under at night. Few of the men were better off …' (Reitz 1999: 117). Later, at a sympathetic farmhouse, he

unearthed an empty grain-bag in which I cut a hole for my head, and one at each corner for my arms, thus providing myself with a serviceable great-coat. My appearance caused much laughter, but I noticed that during the next few days, whenever we passed a barn, grain-bags were in great demand, and soon many of the men were wearing them. (Reitz 1999: 119)

For the Boers the greatest source of resupply was their British enemies and camps and columns were often attacked simply to secure fresh clothing, weapons, ammunition and food. The wearing of captured British uniforms by the Boers became so commonplace that the British issued an order proclaiming

A group of mounted Free State Boers. From the middle of 1900 the character of the war changed, with those commandos still in the field waging hit-and-run warfare against British troops occupying the republics. All the Boers needed to remain in the field were a horse, a gun, ammunition and food; in response the British tried to limit their manoeuvrability with mobile columns of their own and by tying down the veldt with lines of blockhouses, and to deny them a support base among the civilian population by burning farms.

that any Boer captured doing so would be shot. Where the Boers could not forage for themselves they often acquired food from the African population in the countryside, sometimes through trade but often by force. As a result, to add to their difficulties, many such ethnic groups were increasingly hostile to commandos moving through their territory.

For all this there was a strong core of Boer leaders who were determined to resist. In June 1901, despite the efforts of the British cordons, President Steyn met with a number of the most resolute 'bitter-ender' commandants in the western Transvaal, among them De Wet, De la Rey, Botha and Smuts, and it was decided to try to distract the British by taking the war into areas they considered already pacified. While Botha would strike into Natal and Zululand, Smuts would raid into the Cape Colony to support the Cape Boers who had taken to the field there.

Jan Smuts was a determined, dynamic, resolute and occasionally ruthless commander who had been born in the Cape in 1870 but had studied law in the UK and was state attorney for the Transvaal when the war broke out. He had served as a commandant with the Transvaal forces and had excelled in hit-and-run tactics, and by 1901 he was a general. He had perhaps 350 men under his command, most of them young Transvaalers in their early twenties with 18 months' experience behind them, and two lieutenants, Commandant Jacobus van Deventer and Commandant Ben Bouwer. He took no wheeled transport with him but most of the men also led a packhorse and they were accompanied by an unknown number of African grooms.

In order to reach the Cape, Smuts had first to run the gauntlet of the British forces in the Free State. His men crossed the Vaal River in the middle of July 1901, reaching the border with the Cape Colony in the last week of August. Along the way they had brushed several times against the British but had managed to slip away every time, although Smuts lost some 36 men and dozens of horses in the process. Avoiding British patrols guarding the main drifts, Smuts' men crossed the Orange River at Kiba Drift on 4 September but were attacked by BaSothos that same day and narrowly escaped. All the major road and rail routes in the Cape Colony were guarded by the British, and as news of Smuts' arrival spread, columns were organized to search for him. On one occasion, scouting ahead with three men, Smuts was ambushed by a British patrol and was the only man to escape alive. The commando was almost trapped on the Stormberg mountain, but a sympathetic farmer led them at night down a steep pass in the dark and they escaped. They regularly rode 30–40 miles at a stretch, sometimes through the night, snatching what rest they could when there seemed no British were near. By now even the weather had turned against them; the nights were bitterly cold and there were frequent chilling downpours. 'We went floundering ankle-deep in mud and water', remembered Reitz, 'our poor weakened horses stumbling and slipping at every turn; the rain beat down on us, and the cold was awful' (Reitz 1999: 125). When men were wounded in the constant skirmishing there were no medical supplies to treat them and they either had to ride on or were abandoned for the British to find and care for. Dozens more horses died.

Meanwhile the British were closing in. A column of mainly Colonial troops under the command of Lieutenant-Colonel Graham Gorringe was in pursuit, while Lieutenant-Colonel Douglas Haig had ordered the 17th Lancers to move

Members of the Imperial Yeomanry in the field. As British troops across the Army adopted a largely universal and practical uniform – khaki trousers, jacket, slouch hat and bandoliers – and hard-pressed 'bitter-enders' recycled captured British uniforms, it became increasingly difficult to tell the two sides apart. Even a smart Regular cavalry unit such as the 17th (Duke of Cambridge's Own) Lancers had swapped headgear and given up their lances, swords and carbines for Lee-Enfield rifles.

by train from Stormberg to the town of Tarkastad to head off Smuts' advance. They had arrived on 15 September and been deployed along a 9-mile line of the Elands River. They were distributed in squadrons to cover the likely crossing points and C Squadron, under Captain V.S. Sandeman, had occupied a farm called Modderfontein. Sandeman had intended to cross the river, but it was full after the recent rains and instead he camped on the near-side. Modderfontein consisted of a solitary farmhouse and a nearby oblong, well-built, stone cattle-kraal lying in an open valley surrounded by long flat-topped mountains. It was typical Karoo terrain, hard stony ground covered with coarse grass and scattered bush, and a low outcrop of dolerite ran across the property. On the far side the outcrop was only 6½ft high but on the near side it was closer to 20ft and Sandeman instructed his men to place their tents in the lee of the deeper slope. He had with him a mountain gun and a Maxim machine gun from 4 (Mountain) Battery, Royal Garrison Artillery, under the command of Lieutenant P.H. Hay-Coghlan, and these were positioned on top of the rocky outcrop so as to command both the camp and the approaches, and low stone sangars built around them. Sandeman's command totalled around 175 men while A Squadron of the 17th Lancers under Captain N.J. Nickalls was camped a few miles away on a neighbouring farm. The following day, the 16th, Haig himself visited Sandeman to assess his dispositions; he described Sandeman as 'a most capable officer' (quoted in Smith 2004) and made no changes.

The rain had continued intermittently and the morning of Tuesday 17 September was damp and foggy. Sandeman had sent out two patrols into the hills ahead to look for signs of Smuts or of Gorringe's column, but they had seen nothing of either and returned to the camp at Modderfontein. They had not long passed through, however, when a small party of Boer scouts, including Deneys Reitz, had approached from the other direction. At a farm a young man named Jan Coetzer rushed out to warn them of the nearby British presence. Reitz and his companions sent back to Smuts to warn him. Smuts had been hoping to slip past any British cordon unnoticed, but when he rode up now with Van Deventer, Reitz heard him say 'if we did not get those horses and a supply of ammunition we were done for' (Reitz 1999: 126). He decided to attack.

MAP KEY

1   15 September: Following reports that Assistant Commandant-General Jan Christian Smuts' commando is moving towards the Elands River, Captain V.S. Sandeman's C Squadron, 17th Lancers arrive in the Elands valley. The river being swollen by recent rain and preventing Sandeman from occupying the passes into the valley, he establishes his camp close to the river on the Modderfontein farm.

2   Early morning, 17 September: Smuts' men are warned of the British presence by sympathetic farmers. Being short of ammunition and supplies, Smuts decides to attack the Lancers' camp.

3   c.1200hrs, 17 September: Having been alerted by a vedette that Boers have been spotted riding down the valley, Sandeman sends a patrol under Second Lieutenant Philip Russell to investigate. As Russell approaches the bed of a stream he sees figures emerging from the bush along the banks. Thinking they are British, Russell calls out 'Don't fire. We are the 17th Lancers.' The men are Boers, however, and open fire; Russell's men ride back towards the camp.

4   c.1215hrs, 17 September: Russell's men dismount and occupy a rocky rise above the camp. Sandeman had previously placed his artillery (a mountain gun and Maxim machine gun) in rocky emplacements on this ridge.

5   c.1220hrs, 17 September: A party of Boers – including Deneys Reitz – who have been closely pursing Russell's patrol dismount at the foot of the rise and skirmish up it on foot. A fierce firefight then breaks out among the boulders on the summit. Sandeman hurries his men forward from the camp to support the men on the ridge.

6   c.1230hrs, 17 September: A party of Boers under Commandant Ben Bouwer outflanks the British position and captures the farmhouse, raking the camp with fire from the rear.

7   c.1240hrs, 17 September: Having shot down the gun-crews and overrun the summit of the rocky rise, the Boers run down into the camp beyond. A number of Lancers surrender at this point.

8   c.1240hrs, 17 September: A party of Boers led by Smuts himself – who were among the last to arrive on the battlefield at about 1230hrs – occupy a small hill close to the river which outflanks the British left, opening fire on the British rear.

9   c.1245hrs, 17 September: A party of Boers under General Jacobus van Deventer completes the encirclement of the British position.

10   c.1300hrs, 17 September: After continuing to resist despite being surrounded and attacked on all sides, defending a stone cattle-kraal adjacent to the farm, a party of the 17th Lancers finally surrender. The Boers loot the British camp for perhaps 20 minutes before riding on to avoid the arrival of any British reinforcements.

Battlefield environment

In contrast to the grassy terrain of Bothaville, Modderfontein lies on the edges of the Karoo, an area of dry semi-desert where the ground is stony and covered in coarse, dry grass and scrub. The Modderfontein farm lies a few hundred yards from the banks of the Elands River, in a narrow valley surrounded by high, steep, rocky hills. The hills provide a real obstacle for mounted troops trying to cross them and the British strategy at this stage of the war was to try to intercept and contain Smuts' commando by watching the passes through which he might move. Certainly Deneys Reitz, who left the most vivid account of the experiences of Smuts' men, recalled that it was physically challenging riding through such rugged country, and across steep passes – particularly as the weather was bitterly cold and wet – and noted that the commando could not have avoided the British without intelligence from sympathetic farmers who not only reported the British dispositions but guided the Boers down difficult paths.

Modderfontein farm itself nestles in the hollow behind a rocky dolerite ridge just a few feet high which commands the approach road from the north, and which provided the British with an obvious defensive position. Smuts' men had entered the valley of the Elands River to the north by way of a pass and had decided to attack, riding quickly down the narrow valley where a stream flowing into the Elands River and a farm fence provided the only obstacles to slow them. They were aided by misty conditions and by the confusion of the British patrol who at first mistook them for British troops, and indeed much had depended on the speed of their attack because the rocky ridge, had the British not been caught off-guard, would have provided an effective defensive feature. In the event, much of the fighting took place at close quarters among the boulders – a type of fighting at which the Boers excelled, and which denied the British the long-range advantage of their artillery support.

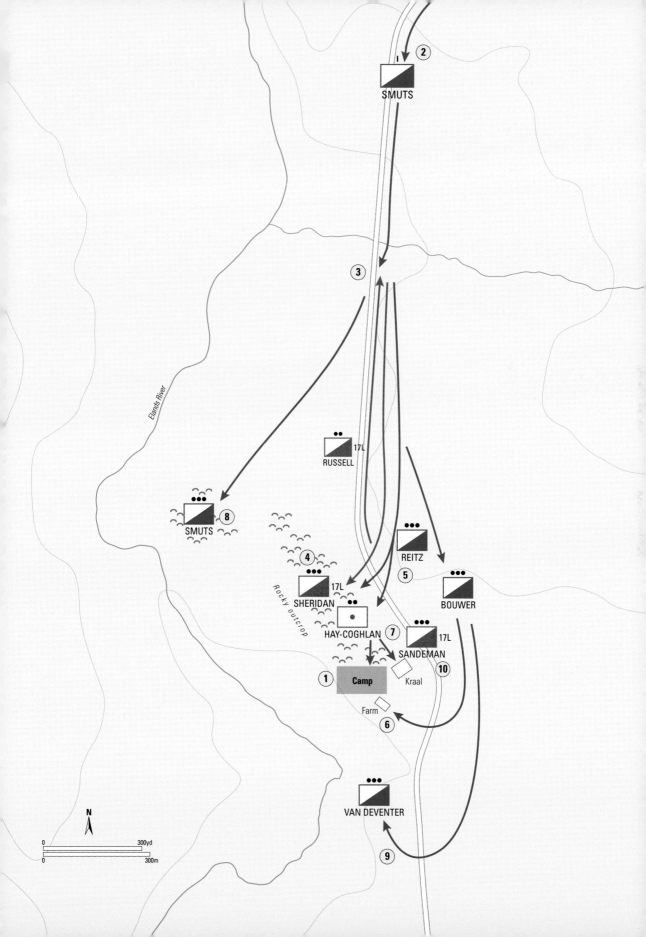

SMUTS ②

③

Elands River

RUSSELL ●●
17L

SMUTS ⑧
●●●

④

Rocky outcrop

SHERIDAN ●●●
17L

REITZ ●●●

⑤

HAY-COGHLAN ●●

⑦

BOUWER ●●●

SANDEMAN ●●●
17L

⑩

① Camp

Kraal

Farm

⑥

VAN DEVENTER ●●●

⑨

N

0   300yd
0   300m

INTO COMBAT

The hard riding and attrition had reduced Smuts' command to about 250 men, but not all of these were ready for action. Many had lost their horses and carried their saddles on foot while others were wounded or exhausted. Smuts directed Bouwer and Van Deventer to attack the 17th Lancers where they could with the most active men – between 15 and 20 of them, including Reitz – while he assembled those coming up behind, of whom about 60 would later join the battle.

In the British camp, meanwhile, Sandeman had no inkling of the imminent attack. One of his outlying vedettes had spotted the commando descending through the hills and had ridden in with a warning, and just after noon Sandeman had sent out a patrol under Second Lieutenant Philip Russell to investigate. Russell was approaching a small stream fringed with bush when he saw men ahead of him, apparently deploying from the bush, and, thinking they must be Gorringe's men, called out 'Don't fire. We are the 17th Lancers' (Wilson 1902: II.745). Afterwards Douglas Haig was bitter about this mistake, blaming it on the Boers for wearing captured khaki uniforms and the carelessness of British irregulars who 'often fire at one another by mistake' (quoted in Smith 2004). In fact, however, they were Commandant Bouwer's men; according to Reitz

> As we were going through the fringe of thorn trees on the other side we rode straight into fifteen or twenty troopers cantering towards us. Most of our men were still among the trees, but four or five of us were in advance, and when we leaped to the ground the soldiers were not more than ten yards away. Opening fire we brought down several, and the rest turned and galloped back along the road. I fired my last two cartridges here, and my first thought was to run to a dead soldier and seize his rifle and bandolier, abandoning my own rusty weapon, then I rushed for my mare and entered the chase. (Reitz 1999: 126)

The survivors of Russell's patrol raced back to the camp. Their horses were in much better condition than the Boers' and they quickly drew ahead, but suddenly encountered a gate in the farm fence, and as they slowed to pass through the Boers closed up and shot two or three more of them. The rest rushed on to warn the camp. While Van Deventer took some men to the left, Bouwer, Reitz and the rest of the advance guard rode straight towards the dolerite ridge which hid the British position beyond:

> Before we reached their outcrop the soldiers opened fire almost point-blank, and worse still, a mountain-gun unexpectedly fired on us from a point to our left, not thirty yards off, and a machine-gun rattled into action close by. So near was the mountain gun that smoke from the discharge billowed over us, although the shells went wide. It was astonishing that any of us escaped, but owing no doubt to our sudden appearance behind the flying patrol, the firing was wild, and only three men and some horses were down before we reached the rocks in which the soldiers were. Here we, in turn, loosed our horses and ran up, to find ourselves within a few feet of our original quarry and a number of others, who had been posted here before. (Reitz 1999: 126–27)

British mounted infantry foraging at a Boer farm are depicted in this work by C.E. Fripp. The life of non-combatants in the occupied republics was unenviable – liable to be looted by both sides, they were often burned out by the British to deny succour to the 'bitter-enders'. The homeless civilians were then taken into 'concentration camps' where they were vulnerable to epidemics, and civilian losses were high.

Scrambling up through the rocks on the low side, Reitz peered over the crest and was astonished to see Sandeman's camp in the hollow beyond 'less than a stone's throw away, buzzing like a disturbed ant-heap. Officers were shouting orders, and men tumbling out of their tents, some running towards us, others going to the right and left to take their stations' (Reitz 1999: 127).

The survivors of Russell's patrol had deployed along the rise next to Hay-Coghlan's guns and were able to slow that initial attack. Among the rocks, 'where we were facing each other almost at hand-shake, a grim duel began. As the soldiers raised their heads to fire we brought them down, for they were no match for us in the short-range work of this kind, and we killed twelve or thirteen and wounded several more, at a distance of a few yards' (Reitz 1999: 127).

Further to the Boer left, both Van Deventer and Bouwer had tried to push around the 17th Lancers' right flank and had found themselves at the farmhouse. Bouwer at once dismounted his men and rushed into the yard, but a sentry posted there saw them and shot one of the Boers dead. Bouwer's men cleared the farmhouse and pushed forward to where they could fire on Sandeman's right flank. At about this time Smuts also arrived with the remaining able men from the commando. They passed to the right of the outcrop, taking up a position on a low rise beyond from which they, in turn, could fire at Sandeman's left and rear from about 800yd away. Reitz thought this move was timely, as the pressure from the British emerging from the camp to join in the fight on the outcrop was beginning to tell and he felt the Boers were in danger of being overwhelmed. The fire from Smuts' men, however, meant that Sandeman's men 'were forced to take cover and could not surround us' (Reitz 1999: 127).

In the meantime Reitz and a companion, a young Transvaaler named Muller, had neutralized Lieutenant Hay-Coghlan's guns. Crawling through the rocks, Reitz had found himself close to the guns and apparently unnoticed:

By the middle of 1901 the 'bitter-enders' were largely reliant on their British enemies for resupply; here, particularly ragged 'bitter-enders' pick over an abandoned British bivouac in search of discarded food, equipment, or dropped cartridges.

… they did not seem to realise that we were so near, for they were unconcernedly loading and firing at our men on the hill six hundred yards back. Standing behind the gun was a tall man handing shells to the three at the breech. I fired at him, and he spun round and sank into a sitting position against the wheel, where I found him dead when the fight was over. The other three ran for the camp at their backs. I fired at one, and he pitched forward dead, while Muller brought down a third, but the last man got away among the tents. (Reitz 1999: 127)

The outcome of the battle now hung on the struggle for the summit of the rocky outcrop – a fierce, quick firefight at close range, a type of fighting which had come to characterize many of the engagements of the guerrilla war. Both sides were mounted men but fighting on foot and neither side lacked courage, although the Boers were more skilful and more experienced:

Nicholas Swart was by my side and shot two other soldiers in quick succession, as they tried to join those in the rocks. There was a young lieutenant a few feet from me. I found out afterwards his name was Sheridan, and they said he was a cousin of Winston Churchill. Twice he rose to fire at me and missed; at his second attempt I grazed his temple, and he dropped out of sight, but only dazed, for in a moment he was up again, swaying unsteadily on his feet, with his face streaming with blood, but still trying to level his rifle at me. While I was hesitating what to do Jack Borrius shot him through the brain. Another soldier fired several rounds at me, and I put a bullet into his head, which was protruding from behind the rock near which he was lying. The sudden shock made him leap up, and again Jack Borrius, who was wonderfully quick, shot him dead as he rose. (Reitz 1999: 127–28)

It was at this stage of the battle that a further British patrol was spotted off to the south. These were men of A Squadron, 17th Lancers who had been sent out from their camp on the neighbouring farm to investigate the sounds of fighting. For the Boers it was not at all clear whether this was a small party or in fact the vanguard of a relief column, and among the rocks they decided to risk an attack on the defenders before the newcomers arrived:

> After a whispered consultation from man to man, Jack Borrius gave the signal, and, rising together, we leaped in among the surviving soldiers. There were only ten to fifteen left, and so far as I can remember not a shot was fired on either side. Our sudden onslaught took them unprepared, and they surrendered at once. Without troubling about our prisoners we ran down shouting and cheering into the camp, before the rest of the defenders knew what had happened. When they saw us among the tents in their rear, something like a stampede set in. Soldiers went running away in all directions, some making away into the thorn trees, others coming towards us and throwing down their arms. One man rushed to the horselines, and mounting barebacked, flourished a revolver and tried to ride off. I shouted to him to halt, but as he gave no heed I shot him dead. (Reitz 1999: 128)

The sudden Boer rush – across just a few yards of ground – certainly took the defenders of the rocky outcrop by surprise and reflected the fact that during the guerrilla phase the commandos were made up of men who were not only young and determined but also desperate; during the conventional

Assistant Commandant-General Jan Smuts (seated centre, flanked by General Jacobus van Deventer, on his right with the riding crop, and General Manie Maritz, on his left) and other members of his commando which raided the Cape at the end of 1901. Smuts imposed an uncharacteristic degree of military-style discipline on his commando, some of which is reflected in their appearance here – and at least two men on the right appear to be wearing captured British uniforms, an offence which the British punished by death.

The British artist Richard Caton-Woodville, Jr (1856–1927) depicted the battle of Modderfontein as a classic colonial 'last stand', with officers and men of the 17th Lancers standing back to back and surrounded. In fact the battle was fought out among the rocks and stone kraals of the Modderfontein farm, and the Lancers had by this stage of the war abandoned both their helmets and lances (foreground). (DEA PICTURE LIBRARY)

phase the burghers had often shied away from close-quarter combat, leaving the advantage in such circumstances to the British.

As Reitz and his companions entered the tents it seemed that the battle was over. In fact, the large stone cattle-kraal lay behind the tents and here Captain Sandeman had rallied a few men. They had suffered from Smuts' telling crossfire and Sandeman himself might have been wounded by this point but, to Reitz's surprise as he peered over the wall, they were not yet ready to surrender:

> We called out 'Hands up! Hands up!' but they turned instead and blazed a volley into our faces. Only our eyes were showing or we should both have been shot. Conradi killed one man and wounded another with a single bullet, and I wounded one, but even now they did not surrender, for, rushing across the kraal, they ranged themselves against the near wall, which alone separated us, and one of them thrust his rifle so near my face that his shot scorched my cheek and neck with cordite, fragments of which had to be picked out for days afterwards, with the point of a knife. When I seized the muzzle he gave an oath and jerked it back so forcibly that the sharp foresight gashed the ball of my thumb and the palm of my hand, and I had to let go. (Reitz 1999: 128)

The sound of the firing attracted the attention of other Boers, however, and as they hurried over the Lancers in the kraal finally decided to give up, throwing their rifles over the wall. Even so, as Reitz turned around the wall looking for the entrance to the kraal he bumped into a Lancer who was working his way in the opposite direction, hoping to catch Reitz's party in the flank. Reitz had the drop on him and the Lancer commented with a grin that the Boer was a 'surprise packet' and surrendered (Reitz 1999: 128).

The battle was now largely over. One small party of Lancers had managed to retreat through a defile to the south, but most of the survivors in the camp had surrendered. The detachment from A Squadron was too small to offer much assistance beyond firing a few shots from a distance. Nevertheless, the Boers realized that they had only a brief window to loot the camp to secure the supplies – the object of the attack – before British reinforcements did arrive. They ransacked the tents and forced many of the prisoners to strip, taking Lancer uniforms to replace their own worn-out clothing. Reitz says that he found Second Lieutenant Lord Vivian lying wounded among the rocks on the outcrop, and that Vivian pointed out a small bivouac tent and suggested it might be worth Reitz looking there:

> I was not slow to take the hint, with the result that having started the morning with a grain-bag for my chief garment, a foundered horse, an old rifle, and two cartridges, I now appeared in a handsome cavalry tunic, riding-breeches, etc., with a sporting Lee-Metford, full bandoliers and a superb mount, a little grey Arab ... I also selected a strong riding mule in preference to another horse, for my experience during the past fortnight had taught me that a good mule for long marches and a light nimble pony for use in action, were the ideal combination ... (Reitz 1999: 129)

There had in fact been upwards of 300 horses and mules in the 17th Lancers' camp and although some of these had been killed or wounded during the

fighting, the men of the commando were largely able to replenish their needs. There was plenty of ammunition and food, too, and the Boers took what they could. Van Deventer – who had started the war as a gunner in the Transvaal Artillery – disabled the mountain gun and the Boers at first carried away the Maxim machine gun. (It proved too cumbersome for their challenging marches, however, and they soon abandoned it in the first dam they came across.) Then they set fire to the tents and whatever else they could, and rode on.

Later, Smuts himself commented, 'How gallantly those boys fought against us, many being killed because they knew not how to surrender' (quoted in Smith 2004). Captain Sandeman and Second Lieutenant Lord Vivian survived their wounds, but British losses were heavy: four officers and 34 men killed and 29 men wounded. Boer losses were one man killed and six wounded.

Watching the Boers loot the camp from a distance, the patrol from A Squadron had immediately sent back for help and at about 1745hrs Haig had arrived from Tarkastad at the head of two Lancer squadrons. In the manner of all the best mounted raiders, Smuts' men had long since vanished over the hills, and all Haig could do was tend to the wounded men. The Boers had made no attempt to take away their prisoners and had merely left them unarmed and stripped of their uniforms.

Smuts was to continue his raid deep into the Cape Colony over the following months, eventually penetrating as far as Okiep, near the west coast. While a handful of Boers did rally to join him, and Afrikaner farms gave him succour along the way, the majority of the Cape Boers were already convinced that the republics could not win the war, and there was no general uprising. Several times members of his commando were captured wearing British uniforms, from the 17th Lancers and others, and some of them were indeed shot. Nevertheless his raid, and the action at Modderfontein – a duel between two cavalry forces, despite the fact that much of it was fought out on foot – was perhaps the supreme example of Boer fighting techniques at their best, of their endurance, resolution, courage and mobility.

Analysis

At the end of 1880, on the eve of the First Anglo-Boer War, the British had been confident that the widely scattered population of civilian farmers, the Boers, could offer them no serious military challenge. In retrospect it is easy to see this as Imperial hubris, and yet it was a view which rested in the end on a professional appreciation of the qualities of the opposing sides. The British were, after all, a global superpower at the time; their Army was thoroughly professional by the standards of the day, they were trained and equipped with the best weapons an advanced industrial economy had to offer, and both their officers and men were experienced in a wealth of colonial warfare. Although Colley himself had not commanded an independent force in action before, he had served in campaigns in China and West Africa and most of the officers and men under his command were veterans of the Zulu campaign. In contrast, the Boer republics possessed only a limited military organization – the commando system – and had no great tradition of discipline; their recent military experience was limited to African enemies and had, indeed, been largely unsuccessful.

It became painfully obvious in just a few weeks, however, that this assessment failed to take account not only of the Boers' less-obvious strengths but of the changing nature of warfare itself. The Boers were determined to the point of stubbornness, and while they lacked the regimental *esprit de corps* which stiffened the backbone of the British military system they were deeply attached to their way of life and, having once taken up arms, were unlikely to be dissuaded by the moral effect of a British bayonet charge. They were much more at home in the southern African terrain than were the British who, in 1881, were still painfully conspicuous in their red coats. Nothing perhaps better demonstrated the changing nature of warfare than the charge of the 58th Regiment at Laing's Nek, who advanced in a style which had proved successful in successive battles since the Napoleonic Wars – in a column with their Colours flying. This was the first time that they had faced an enemy equipped with similar weapons to themselves since the Crimean War of the 1850s, and the 58th Regiment had been so exposed to well-directed small-arms fire from a concealed enemy that not only were they shot to pieces and the attack failed, but the Army ceased thereafter to carry Colours in battle because they attracted so much fire that they were no longer appropriate in modern warfare.

The limited nature of the fighting in 1881 did not reveal the full strengths of Boer tactics. Only at Ingogo was there a hint of the advantages they enjoyed in mobility; in many ways, Smit's attack – approaching the British position on horseback then dismounting to skirmish forward on foot, the men taking advantage of whatever cover they could find and picking their targets until they had secured a fire supremacy over the battlefield – established a blueprint for how such attacks might succeed in the future. Although Colley and his men met it with courage, the British lost the initiative early in the battle and only regained it with their daring escape from the battlefield under cover of darkness at the end. There would be no more opportunities for the Boers to demonstrate their mobility in 1881 although the final battle at Majuba (27 February 1881) – where the Boers skirmished up the slopes of the mountain in groups, supporting one another with covering fire – again demonstrated their skills at using both the ground and their firepower to good effect.

The fate of the Mounted Squadron in 1881 also demonstrated an early failure on the part of the British to recognize how their traditional cavalry tactics should be adapted to the circumstances. Colley, like many Victorian generals, was woefully short of mounted troops but, at a time when the advantages of mounted-infantry warfare were just coming to be recognized, he had not deployed them as such but had used them instead as 'cut-price cavalry' – a role for which they were largely untrained. If they had been deployed at Laing's Nek and had skirmished forward on foot they might have stood some chance of turning the Boer left flank; instead, by attempting a charge up a steep hill they both exhausted their horses and suffered the same fate as the 58th Regiment. The incident at Ingogo, although brief, merely underscored

The Ingogo battlefield after the fight. This photo shows not only the slope of the ground, but also the rocky outcrops behind which both British and Boers took cover. In the foreground are the skeletons of horses which bear witness to the vulnerability of both the Mounted Squadron and gun-teams during the battle.

the point – in attempting to deploy at close range they were destroyed by Boer rifle-fire even before they could attempt to mount an attack.

Colley's death on Majuba Hill and the collapse of British political will to pursue the war left these tactical challenges unresolved and they therefore continued to dominate the battlefield during the conventional phase of the Second Anglo-Boer War. In a number of battles – Talana, Colenso, Magersfontein – the Boers again adopted a defensive strategy, occupying natural features which provided an open killing zone on the approaches, and the distribution of magazine rifles firing smokeless powder greatly improved the volume of fire and the Boers' ability to remain undetected. If the British reluctance to abandon their assumptions of professional superiority seems curious in the light of the evidence from 1881, it is clear that many British commanders in 1899 had dismissed Colley's failures as the result of inexperience and lack of resources. The British military commitment in 1899 was far greater, and there was a belief that, properly handled, the much greater forces available would be unstoppable. This led to a number of occasions where the British mounted frontal attacks on Boer positions, and which ended with the same result as Laing's Nek.

Although the conventional phase of the war – which was largely over by March 1900 – saw some of the heaviest fighting, it did not define the experience of the war. The Boers, too, had taken to the field in an essentially conservative way, carrying their supplies in their ox-wagons as if they were on trek half a century before. The large concentrations of men around Ladysmith were difficult to feed and the elderly senior commanders – the Transvaal's Commandant-General, Piet Joubert, had held the same position in 1881 – lacked drive and initiative, allowing several strategic opportunities to slip past. Once the British had eventually learned to break the Boer cordons, largely through more skilfully managed combined infantry and artillery attacks, the Boers had little option but to disperse their concentrations. This allowed them to free themselves from their traditional commitment to the ox-wagon and it unleashed their other great asset, their mobility.

When the guerrilla war began the British were slow to adapt. The experience of their mounted troops early in the war had been mixed – there had been the odd conventional success, like the charge at Elangslaagte, but other examples, too, of cavalry failing to thrive in local conditions, and being too inflexible to supply the necessary scouting support or pursuit action; and certainly there were too few of them when faced with an enemy whose entire army could take to horse whenever necessary. The success of French's sweep around the Boer flanks certainly helped break their lines at Kimberley, but it had cost thousands of exhausted horses and largely destroyed the subsequent effectiveness of the cavalry brigade on the western front.

The rise in British mounted-infantry-style units, whether Regulars, Yeomanry, Volunteers or Colonial troops, marked a distinct shift in the nature of the war. It was not achieved easily or quickly, and the wastage of horses among newly raised mounted-infantry units as they earned their experience in the field was horrifying. British mounted units, with their Regular mindset, their need to carry supplies with them, their dependence on horse-holders and their inferior knowledge of the terrain, seldom matched the Boer commandos unit for unit and yet they were able to co-ordinate strategies which, particularly when combined with the network of blockhouses and the desolation of Boer farms, steadily reduced the free country through which the commandos could operate.

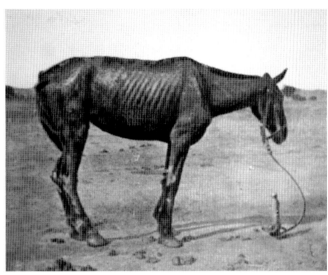

The battle of Bothaville was significant because it demonstrated just how far the British tactical use of mounted troops had come since Ingogo. A relentless pursuit by two British columns had caught even the great De Wet – who had not at that stage abandoned all of his ox-wagons or artillery – off-guard and, having made first contact, the British had hurried up support so quickly that many of De Wet's burghers had panicked. Although De Wet had rallied some of them and they had caused the British real problems by their dogged defence of features around the farm buildings they had not, in the end, been able to withstand the threat of mounted-infantry companies who had deployed in the relative safety of the lee of a low ridge and had then made a determined rush with the bayonet.

The cost in horseflesh of the long, hard drives across the country during the guerrilla war was terrible – this British horse is underfed, overworked and exhausted. At least the British could make good their losses; when the 'bitter-enders' lost horses their only option was to capture new ones from the British.

As the guerrilla war continued the commandos in one sense thrived. Many of the elderly burghers retired from the field and those that were left were the fittest and most committed. Some commandants like Smuts began to impose a stricter discipline on their men, which added to their military efficiency. For the most part without heavy guns or wagons they could cover large distances at a stretch, often achieving considerable feats when exploiting natural features to slip through the British cordons. As Smuts demonstrated during his raid into the Cape these streamlined commandos could still outrun British columns and, taking advantage of intelligence from sympathetic civilians, could mount quick hit-and-run attacks not only to inconvenience the enemy but also to resupply themselves. The 17th Lancers at Modderfontein might have shed many of the conventional trappings with which they had begun the war, but they could not match the Boers in the intense close-quarter firefights which then characterized the fighting.

Yet for all their daring and resolve, most of the bitter-enders came to realize in the end that they were engaged in a war of attrition which they could not win. Without food, fresh horses, clothing, ammunition and even medical supplies – they habitually abandoned their wounded knowing that the British would capture and treat them – they needed to fight constant skirmishes to win what they needed from their enemy but which, it was increasingly obvious, were not affecting the outcome of the war. Cumbersome though they were, the British were steadily tying down the veldt and depriving the Boers not only of civilian support but of their last great asset, their mobility. In this regard, although it was a far cry from the *arme blanche* so beloved of cavalry theorists, the contribution of British mounted troops to the outcome of the war was immense.

Aftermath

After the action at Modderfontein, Smuts continued his long ride across the northern Cape and at the beginning of April 1902 laid siege to the British garrison at the copper-mining town of Okiep in Namaqualand. Since he had crossed the Vaal heading south at the beginning of August 1901, he and his men had ridden thousands of miles, fought dozens of actions, and tied down thousands of British troops in pursuit. They had inflicted far more casualties and damage than they had suffered themselves, yet it had become increasingly clear that they were having no effect on the outcome of the war. There was no widespread rising of 'Cape rebels', and elsewhere the old Boer republics were on the verge of collapse. Other Boer guerrilla commandants, no less resolute than Smuts – De la Rey, De Wet, Botha – had continued to trouble the British with the same strategy of hit-and-run attacks, but the British response was taking a heavy toll on the civilian population. Networks of blockhouses and fences criss-crossed both the Transvaal and Free State and, while the British columns never achieved the degree of mobility attained by the 'bitter-ender' commandos, they were becoming steadily more proficient – and there were many more of them. Food, ammunition and even horses were in critically short supply for the Boers. 'Nothing could have proved more clearly how nearly the Boer cause was spent', wrote Reitz, 'than these starving, ragged men clad in skins or sacking, their bodies covered in sores, from lack of salt or food, and their appearance was a great shock to us, who came from the better-conditioned forces in the Cape' (Reitz 1999: 178).

The British practice of cutting off serving commandos from their support base in the civilian community by destroying farms and removing non-combatants to camps had taken a terrible toll. Large areas of the former republics had been reduced to a wasteland, with homes burnt and crops destroyed, while the concentration of Boer non-combatants in camps had led to thousands of deaths from disease. Moreover, the indigenous population, who had borne the brunt of the bitter-enders' foraging expeditions, had become increasingly willing to take up arms. By remaining in the field the commandos risked not only a slow but inevitable destruction of their remaining military manpower, but also grave consequences for the Afrikaner civilian population. By May 1902 leading Boer representatives, including commandants of bitter-ender commandos, were prepared to consider opening peace negotiations with the British, and an attack by the Zulu on a commando at Holkrans, in northern Natal, on 6 May added impetus to the movement. On 31 May the Boer representatives signed the Treaty of Vereeniging under which they agreed to lay down their arms on condition that there would be no retribution against those who had fought and that the republics would one day be allowed to govern themselves again. The British abandoned their former insistence that black Africans be allowed a limited franchise. While the treaty brought the war to an end, it also paved the way for future struggles; in 1910 the former British colonies and Boer republics were united as the Union of South Africa – both Botha and Smuts would become Presidents – but a rise in Afrikaner nationalism, fuelled by memories of the war, led to increasingly oppressive policies towards the indigenous population and the birth of apartheid.

The bitter end: burghers surrendering at the close of hostilities in May 1902. The long years of war have taken their toll on their appearance – the boy sitting on the right is wearing a blanket as a cape against the weather – and while the piled weapons still include a number of Mauser rifles, most are British weapons.

For the British, however, the lessons of victory were mixed. Mounted-infantry warfare had certainly come to dominate the fighting and in the initial aftermath of the war there was a move to step up mounted-infantry training based at Aldershot. Yet the war had also highlighted the earlier debate about the role and nature of cavalry – not only was it argued that the Second Anglo-Boer War was the product of a unique combination of circumstances and terrain, but powerful factions argued that rival European powers still maintained large conventional cavalry forces. Rather than the widespread adoption of mounted-infantry tactics there was, instead, a conservative shift towards restoring the role of the cavalry as a shock force. In 1907 the lance – abandoned during the Second Anglo-Boer War – was re-introduced and although mounted-infantry companies were deployed in Somaliland in 1903, the mounted-infantry training school in Aldershot was closed down in 1913. Mounted infantry officially ceased to be a part of the British Army. In the event, conventional cavalry tactics did not long survive the outbreak of World War I in 1914, although it is unlikely that, in the face of increasingly mechanized warfare, mounted-infantry companies would have found an enduring role any more than did the cavalry.

UNIT ORGANIZATIONS

Boer commando

Since Boer commandos were essentially a part-time militia, their numbers fluctuated according to the level of the civilian population. In 1899 the largest, the Pretoria commando, numbered 2,832 men while the smallest, from Thaba Nchu, just 98 – most numbered in their hundreds. In peacetime each civilian district was governed by a *landdrost* (magistrate) assisted by several *veld-kornette* (field cornets), and during wartime the associated commando elected its own *kommandant* (commandant) while the field cornets served as junior officers. In addition, each group of burghers who camped together elected a *korporaal* (corporal) from among their own ranks.

At the beginning of most campaigns the commandant was usually a man of considerable social standing; as wars progressed, however, commandants who proved inept or ineffectual were often voted out and younger men of proven military capability elected to replace them. Senior commanders – ranked as *kommandant-generaal* (commandant-general) or *veg-generaal* (fighting general) – were appointed by the republics to direct operations as a whole.

A montage of Boer leaders of the First Anglo-Boer War.

British units

Mounted-infantry companies were envisaged to have a paper strength of 133 of all ranks. Ideally, this consisted of one commanding officer (major or captain), four lieutenants, one sergeant-major, five sergeants, six corporals, two sergeant-farriers, four shoeing-smiths, two buglers, 97 privates, five dismounted men (officers' servants), five cooks and waggoneers and one saddler. Each infantry battalion was required to submit a detachment of men for mounted-infantry training at Aldershot; after training, these men returned to their parent battalions, but could be assembled to form companies when required. This then happened at the beginning of the Second Anglo-Boer War – each mounted-infantry company therefore consisted of trained men drawn from a number of infantry battalions. They would serve together throughout the war as the companies were in fact deployed as permanent tactical units, although of course many companies in the field were under-strength due to attrition of both men and horses.

The establishment of a British Regular cavalry regiment remained largely unchanged across the period 1881–1902. A regiment consisted of about 650 officers and men, including the regimental headquarters (lieutenant-colonel and major and staff), paymaster, quartermaster, medical officer and artificers (saddlers, farriers, shoeing-smiths, etc.), and was divided into four squadrons. Each squadron consisted of two captains, four lieutenants, two troop sergeant-majors, six sergeants, eight corporals, four artificers, two trumpeters, 120 privates and two drivers. In the field these numbers were often reduced by casualties, sickness and by men on detached duties, so that a squadron on a given occasion might number only 90–100 men. More were rendered ineffective by the heavy wastage of horses while campaigning in South Africa due to the harsh terrain, poor pasture, long distances travelled and over-work.

The raising of Imperial Yeomanry units was authorized in December 1899. County Yeomanry regiments had been raised for local defence only and could not serve outside the UK, but the Imperial Yeomanry were authorized to draw a core of recruits (roughly one-third) from existing Yeomanry units and to make up the remainder from suitable volunteers. An Imperial Yeomanry company retained its county affiliations and consisted nominally of 121 men, and a number of companies were combined to form a battalion. Early battalions varied between five and eight companies although the last detachments, formed in 1901, were generally standardized as four companies.

BIBLIOGRAPHY

Amery, L.S., ed. (1900–09). *The Times History of the War in South Africa*. London: Sampson Low, Marston.

Anglesey, Marquess of (1986). *A History of the British Cavalry, Vol. 4: 1899–1913*. London: Leo Cooper.

Boyden, Peter B., Guy, Alan J. & Harding, Marion (1999). *Ashes And Blood; The British Army In South Africa 1795–1914*. London: National Army Museum.

Butler, Lieutenant-General Sir William (1899). *The Life of Sir George Pomeroy-Colley*. London: John Murray.

Carter, Thomas F. (1900). *A Narrative of the Boer War: Its Causes and Results*. London: John McQueen.

Carver, Field Marshal Lord Michael (1999). *The National Army Museum Book of the Boer War*. London: Sidgwick & Jackson.

Castle, Ian (1996). *Majuba 1881: The Hill of Destiny*. Campaign 45. Oxford: Osprey Publishing.

Crouch, John & Knight, Ian, eds (1981). *Forged In Strong Fires: The Transvaal War of 1881, A.V.M.S. Centenary Publication*. London: Victorian Military Society.

De Wet, Christiaan (1902). *Three Years War*. London: Archibald Constable.

Duxbury, George R. (1981). *David and Goliath: The First War of Independence 1880–81*. Johannesburg: South African Museum of Military History.

Emery, Frank (1986). *Marching Over Africa: Letters from Victorian Soldiers*. London: Hodder & Stoughton.

Knight, Ian (1996a). *Go to your God like a Soldier: The British Soldier Fighting for Empire 1837–1902*. London: Greenhill.

Knight, Ian (1996b). *Boer Wars (1): 1836–1898*. Men-at-Arms 301. Oxford: Osprey Publishing.

Knight, Ian (1996c). *Boer Wars (2): 1898–1902*. Men-at-Arms 303. Oxford: Osprey Publishing.

Knight, Ian (2004). *Boer Commando 1876–1902*. Warrior 86. Oxford: Osprey Publishing.

Laband, John (2005). *The Transvaal Rebellion: The First Boer War*. London: Pearson.

Lehmann, Joseph (1972). *The First Boer War*. London: Jonathan Cape.

Meintjes, Johannes (1971). *The Commandant-General: The Life and Times of Petrus Jacobus Joubert*. Cape Town: Tafelberg.

Norris-Newman, C.L. (1882). *With the Boers in the Transvaal and Orange Free State in 1880–1*. London: W.H. Allen.

Pakenham, Thomas (1979). *The Boer War*. London: Weidenfeld & Nicolson.

Pretorius, Fransjohan (1999). *Life on Commando During the Anglo-Boer War 1899–1902*. Cape Town: Humand & Rousseau.

Reitz, Deneys (1999). *Adrift on the Open Veld: The Anglo-Boer War and its Aftermath*. Cape Town: Stormberg.

St. Leger, Stratford (1986). *Mounted Infantry at War; Boer War Sketches*. Johannesburg: Galago Publishing.

Shearing, Taffy & David (2000). *General Smuts and his Long Ride*. Sedgefield: privately published.

Smith, R.J. (2004). 'Modderfontein, 17 September 1901', *Military History Journal*, Vol. 13, No. 1. Available at http://samilitaryhistory.org/vol131rs.html

Various authors (1981). *First War of Independence 1880–81 Centenary Issue*. Military History Journal. Johannesburg: South African Military History Society.

Wilson, H.W. (1899–1900). *With The Flag to Pretoria*. 2 vols. London: Harmsworth Brothers.

Wilson, H.W. (1902). *After Pretoria: The Guerrilla War*. 2 vols. London: The Amalgamated Press.

Officers of the 17th (Duke of Cambridge's Own) Lancers, photographed in 1899. The early stages of the war were not kind to Regular cavalry units, whose professional expertise was not best suited to campaigning on the veldt; even by this stage the uniforms are largely devoid of regimental or rank badges, and by 1901 the helmets had been replaced with slouch hats and the lances with rifles and bandoliers, the shock tactics of the mounted cavalry charge having given way to mounted-infantry warfare.

INDEX

References to illustrations are shown in **bold**.
References to plates are shown in bold with caption pages in brackets, e.g. **38–39**, (40).